ROE DEER

Recent Books by Richard Prior

Modern Roe Stalking (Tideline) 1985
Game Management in Small Woodlands (Game Conservancy) 1987
Roe Stalking (Game Conservancy) 1987
L'Approche du Chevreuil (Gerfaut Club) 1987
Deer Watch (Swan Hill Press) 1993
Trees & Deer (Swan Hill Press) 1994
The Roe Deer (Swan Hill Press) 1995

ROE DEER

Management and Stalking

RICHARD PRIOR

SWAN·HILL PRESS

First published in the UK in 2000
by Swan Hill Press
Reprinted 2003

British Library Cataloguing-in-Publication Data
  A catalogue record for this book
  is available from the British Library

ISBN 1 84037 138 2

Typeset by Rowland Phototypesetting, Bury St Edmunds, Suffolk
Printed in China

Swan Hill Press
an imprint of Quiller Publishing Ltd
Wykey House, Wykey, Shrewsbury, SY4 1JA, England
E-mail: info@quillerbooks.com
Website: www.swanhillbooks.com

Acknowledgements

Photographs make or break a book, and I am once again indebted to Bruce Potts of Sylvan Films, Joop Poutsma, Mike Swan (Game Conservancy), John Penfold, Dominic Griffith, Robin Lowes and Allan Allison for permission to use their superb pictures. Others come from my own collection, though not necessarily taken by myself. As some of them are unidentified, all I can do is thank the photographers and apologise for not being able to ask their permission. The line drawings are by my old friend Jeppe Ebdrup and the distribution map was kindly supplied by the Game Conservancy Trust.

Some items for this book has been taken from its predecessor, *Roe Stalking*, published by the Game Conservancy, others from occasional writings with the kind permission of the editors of *Shooting Times* and *Stalking Magazine*. I am very grateful to Dominic Griffith for reading through my text and bringing it up to date where I have been more than usually old-fashioned. Also to John Clifton-Bligh for his masterly summary of the perils a stalker faces under the Health & Safety and other well-intentioned but onerous regulations. Mark Hatt-Cook very kindly checked the complexities of stalking law.

Contents

Foreword

The knowledge and practice of woodland deer management has progressed a long way since the bad old days of deer drives and snaring. Though still a potential or actual pest, scientific research has increased our understanding of the deer themselves, and the skills of humane management and stalking with the rifle are now taught through courses at different levels organised by the British Deer Society, the British Association for Shooting and Conservation, the Forestry Commission and the St Hubert Club. We all have to keep abreast of the latest developments, so the material in this book has been revised and updated as far as possible to conform with the syllabus leading up to the Deer Stalking Certificate, Levels 1 and 2 administered by Deer Management Qualifications Ltd. Their address will be found in Appendix 5.

Roe are charming creatures, but they are pests to forestry and farming and have few enemies to control their numbers. *(Photo Sylvan Films)*

PART 1

Introducing Roe Stalking

Woodland deer stalking is rather like wildfowling; one is pitting one's wits against a totally wild quarry, relying for success on knowledge of their habits. The more you understand the day-to-day life of the particular species you are after, the better chance you have.

Deer are very adaptable animals, varying their habits according to the food available at the time, the amount of human disturbance (and stalking is a very significant element in that) as well as their own biological needs. The more you understand how they are likely to behave, the nearer success you will be.

Most deer have learned that humans, their greatest enemy, are most active during the day, and so they move and feed primarily at dusk and dawn. One of the earliest lessons which a stalker has to accept is that he has to forget about the normal conventions of human life, suiting his hours to the deer, not to regular meal times or the other tedious requirements of what other, unenlightened people think are the essentials of human behaviour. For a teenager still living at home a conscious effort may have to be made to break away from family routines so that he can leave the house without friction in the small hours, refining his technique to avoid waking everyone, and again coming home late without problems.

The Bambi factor

Take up deer stalking and you are bound to be faced with the ethical question of whether you are justified in taking the life of a beautiful animal. Sooner or later every stalker needs to be happy in his own mind about the rationale behind deer control, even if he is not faced with doubts on the part of his own family, friends and neighbours, not to speak of any anti-sport enthusiasts he may meet.

Luckily, nobody in possession of the real facts can doubt that deer numbers in this country have to be kept within limits. Deer may be an important component in our fauna but they are also potential pests. They damage or interfere with a variety of essential human activities – forestry, farming and gardening in particular. Unlike so many forms of vanishing wildlife that we see on the telly, deer are highly successful and adaptable creatures, in no way threatened by life in an overcrowded, industrialised island. Nor can they be confined by a stroke of any official pen to some sort of utopian 'reserve' where they might be allowed to live and reproduce in primeval bliss. As many suburban garden-owners know all too well, there are few counties, if any, where deer of one or several species cannot be expected to turn up one time or another. Nearly everywhere they are an ever-present menace.

We almost certainly have more than one million deer living wild in Britain – nobody knows the real figure – and taking one species with another, there are certainly 300,000 little Bambis born every year. What happens to them? Our farming, forestry and garden crops provide food in abundance, but the natural enemies which once limited their numbers have long ago been eliminated: the wolf about 1745; the wild boar, the lynx and the bear long before. If we don't take a hand, nature in the form of disease and starvation will do the job well enough, but not before the deer have done unacceptable damage not only to crops, but to their own – and our – environment.

All right, the environmentalists say, let us reintroduce the wolf and let natural predation re-establish the so-called Balance of Nature – wolves are claimed to be as harmless to man as teddy-bears. Harmless they may be, but they are certainly not fools, and deer are more trouble to catch than stupid sheep – or a pony in its paddock.

For their own health, and to ensure that deer have their rightful place in our countryside, control is essential. What makes the difference between greedy, possibly cruel sport-shooting and proper deer management is whether we just go out to kill a buck, the bigger the better, or if our shooting decisions are soundly based on a plan which recognises the place of deer in the country-side in relation to all other activities, promotes the wellbeing of the herd as an entity, and in its execution is as humane as skill and training can make it.

Any stalker is well advised these days to keep a low profile and to be reasonably unobtrusive to the public gaze. That does not mean he has in any way to be ashamed of the real down-to-earth conservation work which he does.

Part 2

Know Your Quarry

Identification

The six species of deer found wild in Britain fall into two groups. Red, fallow and sika deer are large in size, form herds and are relatively unselective feeders. Roe, with muntjac and Chinese water deer, are small, rarely form more than family groups, and need richer food sources. The new shoots of trees, shrubs and low plants form a very important part of their diet. Roe have a shoulder height of 65–73 cm (26–29 in), compared to fallow bucks 90–95 cm (35–37 in), fallow does 80–85 cm (31–33 in) and muntjac only 43–46 cm (17–18 in).

The live weight of a mature roe varies between 23 and 32 kg (50–70 lb), according to the food supply. Carcass weights (eviscerated, head and legs off) from 10 to 25 kg (22–55 lb) upwards are more usually quoted. There is no great difference in size between the sexes. Most people overestimate the size and weight of the deer they see because they have fine bones and long legs for their size.

A roe buck in summer coat.

A doe in winter coat. Note the gorget patches of white on the throat. *(Photo J Poutsma)*

Seeing roe, particularly in thick winter coat, makes it difficult to imagine that they weigh less than the average labrador.

In summer roe are chestnut-coloured without spots, individuals varying from sandy to deep red-brown. The vestigial tail is usually invisible but they have a pale perianal (rump) patch, the *target*, which tends to be whitish in Scotland, lemon to pale brown farther

A new-born kid. Their dappled coat and tendency to lie still makes them difficult to spot. *(Photo Sylvan Films)*

south. The nose is black and the chin white. The winter coat is thicker and dark brown to grey in colour, the rump white with the hairs erectile in alarm, giving a powder-puff effect. Sometimes there are one or two paler patches (*gorgets*) on the throat. The winter coat is shed progressively from March to May, animals at this time having a very ragged appearance. In contrast, the winter coat grows tidily through the summer coat around September. New-born kids have a splashed pattern of irregular white spots on a variegated ground of brown and black. The spots fade from August to September but can usually be seen until the growth of the first winter coat.

The mature buck's antlers typically carry six points: brow, top and back point on each side. They are shed annually in the period from October to December, and grow in velvet to March or April when the velvet is removed by fraying, clean antlers being carried through the summer and autumn. Young bucks clean later than adults, some being still in velvet as late as the beginning of June.

Roe can be distinguished from muntjac by their long legs, upright stance, large pointed ears, broad black nose and six-point antlers. Muntjac have a pig-like, hunched silhouette, short antlers on long furry pedicles and a broad tail which is often carried vertically in alarm. The Chinese water deer has prominent canine teeth, a short dark tail, 'button' eyes and nose, and short, rounded ears. Both sexes are antlerless. Fallow are considerably larger and the males have flattened, large antlers. The tail is long and mobile, the coat usually spotted.

Origins and spread

Roe are native to Britain. They were widespread and numerous until Tudor times but then suffered a decline which resulted in their virtual disappearance from England and Wales by the eighteenth century. Even in Scotland at this time they were mostly confined to the Highlands.

Roe were reintroduced to southern England at various centres through the nineteenth century. At the same time they began to recolonise south through Scotland to the English border, where they were reported by 1900. This spread has continued through the twentieth century so that roe of Scottish origin are now found as far south as Sheffield and North Wales. All the southern counties are now populated, from east Cornwall to west Kent. Roe are also reported in the southern and Midland counties and on the Welsh marches, while a colony in Thetford has expanded to occupy a large part of East Anglia (see distribution map on page 18).

Roe distribution in the early 1990s. Blue: areas where roe are currently established. Green: areas where roe are not yet present in significant numbers.
(Map produced from the Countryside Information System (CIS). Copyright Natural Environment Research Council and Department of Environment, Transport and the Regions, with acknowledgements to the Ordnance Survey and the Institute of Terrestrial Ecology, Monks Wood. Mammal data from Arnold, H R (1993) *The Atlas of Mammals in Britain* ITE Research Publication, NERC, HMSO (1993).)

Behaviour

Roe deer are highly successful animals because they are able to adapt to different circumstances. Under conditions where the formation of herds or even long-distance migration is appropriate they are able to change their fundamental behaviour patterns, quite apart from smaller adaptations, so do not expect them to behave in a text-book way! In Britain, however, they mostly conform to a territorial lifestyle. To some extent their behaviour is easy for us to understand because their social organisation is rather similar to our own. Man and roe buck are both territorial animals by preference. The size and location of the territory are determined by an individual's place in the social hierarchy and his ability to defend it from other mature males.

The size of the territory does not depend primarily on population density, but more on food availability and the structure of the habitat, which determines the distance at which the holder can become aware of another buck and feel it necessary to chase him off. In newly afforested areas one territory may extend to a nearby skyline. A few years later two or three hectares may be sufficient for a buck because the trees have grown up until he is unable to see 50 metres. Some elbow room is necessary, but territories in thick cover with sufficient food tend to be small. Once the boundaries have been decided in spring, often with much threat display of barking and fraying, adjacent territory holders appear to work

Territory marking by scent and demonstration begins before the antlers are clean.

Besides using small trees to remove the velvet, fraying stocks, usually with a scrape below, mark a buck's territory.

out a sort of tolerant gentleman's agreement. A little-used area between them often serves as a no-man's-land through which non-territorial animals can pass without running any serious risks.

Requirements for a mature buck's territory seem to be the availability of food and cover and lack of disturbance, preferably with a sunny clearing. In densely-planted conifer forests where the soil is infertile and sour the richest grazing is often along the stream-bottoms. Major bucks are likely to be attracted to such places and establish their territories there, especially if tree planting has been kept back from the watercourse.

A buck marks his presence along the paths which cross his territory and towards the boundaries by fraying the bark off small trees. He does this by rubbing his antlers up and down, at the same time making a scrape below the tree with his forefoot. Scent is deposited on the fraying stock from the frontal scent glands

Threat forms a major part of territorial behaviour.

located on the forehead, and probably also on the scrape by the interdigital gland between the cleaves of the forefoot. Certainly the buck stamps heavily in his scrape, producing a deeply imprinted footmark which could release the secretion. Contrary to what one might expect, most fraying and scraping is done by young bucks, who have to mark and defend their territory by every possible means. Large bucks of considerable presence are able to assert themselves by deep grunts of aggression and a generally formidable appearance. Naturally the more young bucks there are in the area seeking territories the more the older, established bucks have to defend themselves, and this leads to excessive fraying damage if the forestry plantations are at a vulnerable stage.

The doe, too, defends a territory around the time of fawning. She is almost as aggressive as the buck in chasing out strange females, and in due course her own young of the previous year. A buck's territory may or may not coincide with that of a doe; it may on the other hand take in part or all of another doe's territory. It is, however, simplistic to claim that a buck and a doe living more or less in the same area behave totally independently. There is a degree of mutual association.

In the late spring aggression develops between territorial bucks and male kids of the previous year, now eleven months old. Most of these are chased away to find an unoccupied territory or, failing that, to live a precarious existence with other unsuccessful juveniles of both sexes. They accumulate in places which are not taken up by territorial animals because of lack of cover or constant disturbance. It is significant that buck kids with the heaviest weight at birth are the first to be ejected, presumably because they respond more quickly to the adult buck's aggression. In a fully stocked situation these young bucks have little chance of ever achieving a territory. On the other hand, where the population is expanding and occupying new ground they will be the first colonists and often develop into the finest specimens.

Buck kids of low birth weight are often tolerated by the territorial buck as they offer no direct challenge to his authority. Many remain in the parental territory through their first year as satellite bucks, subservient to the occupier but benefiting at the same time from life in a defended and preferred territory which becomes familiar to them. If the territorial buck is killed, there is a good chance that the satellite buck, because of his knowledge of the territory and his pride of possession, will be able to defend it successfully against other and possibly larger bucks. *Thus, if the population is allowed to become too great the best stock emigrates and is lost, while the worst inherit territories to which, by virtue of their poor development, they are not entitled. When density*

Yearling bucks either wander away from occupied territories or lead a subservient role to the occupier.

rises to a peak, loss of quality in body weight and antler size inevitably follows. The implications of this for management are profound.

The weather has a fundamental effect on behaviour. After a cold night, for example, there will be much free movement as the sun rises. On windy days roe seek the shelter of hedges and dells. After rain they emerge to avoid the drips and dry themselves, and even in the middle of very heavy rainstorms the woods may be full of moving deer as they change their ground.

Feeding

Although roe are ruminants they cannot cope with large quantities of low-quality food. The bulk of their food consists of the highly nutritious buds, leaves and young twigs of trees and bushes, which labels them as browsing animals. Brambles, coppice growth and ivy are the most preferred foods but roe are catholic in their taste and highly adaptable, depending on the habitat. They like a wide variety in their diet and will at times eat hedge fruit, fungi and cereal grains. Deer living on open moorland can exist on heather which, although it is not ideal, provides a reasonable level of nutrition through the year. Heather-feeding roe often have excessive wear on their incisor teeth because they have to nibble although, unlike rodents, they only have incisors in the lower jaw.

Roe are primarily browsing animals, preferring leaves and buds to grass. They can reach up just over one metre. *(Photo J Poutsma)*

Otherwise, when they are feeding on bushes and young trees they often take the twig right into the mouth and chew it off with the molars. They eat grass and corn in spring but only the young growing points attract them. Although they may still be in the fields when the crop has reached 10 cm (4 in) or so in height, they will mainly be feeding on recently germinated weed seedlings. Some apparently useful forage is almost valueless. For example it has been claimed that a diet containing 70 per cent Sitka spruce is actually fatal to roe. Anything out of the ordinary will be sampled, and trees that have recently had a dose of fertiliser will attract them, which possibly explains the fact that nursery transplants are more heavily browsed than naturally regenerated seedlings.

When they graze, roe choose seedlings and new sprouts which are richer than taller growth.

Fallen trees provide fresh browse and can be a magnet for hungry roe.

Roe Deer Timetable

Month	Buck	Doe
March	Feeding in fields Adult bucks in full or dry velvet	Feeding in fields
April	Yearlings cast out Most adult bucks clean Fraying	Yearlings cast out
May	Coat change Bucks in territories Most yearlings clean	Coat change Kids born
June	Some mature bucks move to fields and hedges	Kids start to follow doe
July	First signs of rut	Early rut chases
August	Rut peak 3rd to 10th	Mating
September	Coat change	Coat change Kids weaned
October	Feeding in fields	Feeding in fields
November	Antler cast (older bucks) Movement back to woods	Movement back to woods
December	Antler cast complete	Foetal implantation
January	Older bucks velvet to ears Some kids have buttons	Does visibly pregnant
February	Older bucks in full velvet Kid buttons cast	Increased intensity of feeding

Roe deer tend to feed at dusk and dawn because they have learned that these are periods when they are less likely to be disturbed. Their natural feeding rhythm is, however, quite different. By preference they like to feed at intervals throughout the day, and during the night when there is sufficient moon or starlight. Short periods of feeding are followed by rumination which lasts ten or fifteen minutes. After this a period of repose, but not sleep, may be followed by loafing or limited movement before feeding starts again. Roe very rarely sleep, but they are capable of long periods of inaction without great loss of weight.

In the years since deer stalking has become accepted as the

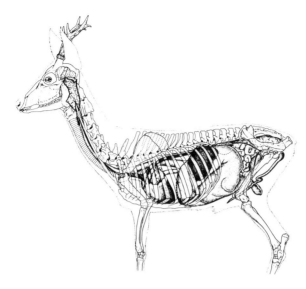

Anatomical drawing showing internal organs in place. *(Courtesy of Professor R R Hofmann)*

normal means of control, roe have learned that dawn and dusk may not now be a safe period but the most dangerous to be moving about. Many observers have recently noted a tendency to feed more during the late morning – after the stalker has gone home for breakfast!

When food is short in the woods, deer congregate on farm crops.

The rut

The first signs of the approaching rut are seen in late June or early July when the bucks become more restless, letting off steam by increased fraying and by barking at other deer. They are seen questing, nose to ground, apparently in pursuit of an interesting doe. In fact the rigid territorial system which the bucks have maintained since the spring tends to break down. Fights between well-matched rivals can occur, although most disputes are settled by barking and a variety of threat displays. It is thought that one doe coming into season is needed to trigger full rutting activity, and this may be the reason for the great difference in the start of the rut proper between areas, and even between one wood and the next. Hectic chases, with the buck following the doe, may be expected from about 20 July onwards with the peak of the rut usually around 5–7 August. During these chases, and at other times when she wants to attract a buck, the doe makes a high-pitched squeaking noise, while he responds with an asthmatic wheezing. Sometimes these chases become centred on some object such as a tree stump, anthill or clump of rushes, and a circular or figure-of-eight track develops, known as a roe ring.

The buck's part is secondary to that of the doe. She selects where she will rut, and lacking a buck she will go and find one, often from

Mating is preceded by long chases, at first very fast, then slowing to a walk. Chases round an object like a bush or stone will make a track known as a roe ring.

some distance, and bring him back. This is a subtle equalising influence on roe populations which is often forgotten about. The object of the chase is probably to accustom both partners to the idea of physical contact which roe, except for siblings, avoid at other times of the year. At the culmination of this courting process the doe allows herself to be mounted and this the buck attempts, often many times before a successful union is achieved. After the first mating a doe may accept the attentions of more than one buck. They are in no way monogamous, though there appears to be some loose form of attachment between a buck and a doe not only during the rut but also at other times. The nature of this pair bond, if it really exists, is so far little understood. The doe is monoestrous, only coming into season once a year.

Rutting activity is most likely to be seen during the day if the weather is warm and dry or thundery. In cold and wet or windy weather there will be little to see and mating probably takes place with a minimum of preliminary play.

The rut dies down very quickly about 12–15 August. For the next two or three weeks the bucks will be very difficult to find. However, individuals may be found continuing to rut into September.

Observers in many countries have noticed that some bucks show signs of rutting activity again much later in the year. This is the so-called false rut, which occurs in Britain around the end of September. There will be a certain resumption of fraying, but only a small proportion of bucks are involved, perhaps one in ten, and one possibility is that these are precocious yearlings. A small number of doe kids have been found to be pregnant in their first autumn and these may also have been involved in this late show of rutting behaviour. Mature bucks have on rare occasions been seen to mate very early in the summer and the birth of kids well outside the normal period is occasionally reported. For example, in 1999 a new-born kid was found in Dorset at the beginning of March.

The breeding calendar of roe is completely different from other species. Red, fallow and sika rut in October to produce young in May or June. The smaller Chinese water deer rut in December to produce fawns born in June or July. Muntjac, which are non-seasonal breeders, also have a gestation of about seven months. Roe are unique in taking nearly ten months between rut and fawning. The reasons for this are obscure, although the mechanism is now well understood. It is known as *delayed implantation*.

The fertilised egg increases only slowly in size, and from August to December remains floating free in the maternal uterus. By mid-December the embryo is still only about 20 mm in length. About Christmas it becomes attached to the wall of the uterus and development after this proceeds at the normal speed. Thus females that are shot in the early part of the winter may appear to be barren, although careful examination of the ovaries will show one or more corpora lutea (yellow bodies) which develop after ovulation.

Fawning

The fawns, or more properly kids, are born between late April and early July, with a peak around 20 May. Where the food supply is adequate most does produce twins every year from the age of two. Triplets are not uncommon, but the chances of all three surviving are small. Some have single kids and this proportion increases with a decline in habitat quality.

Young kids spend most of their time hidden while the doe is feeding, which gives rise to many mistaken claims of kids having been abandoned. If a kid for this reason is picked up and reported, every effort should be made to take it back to the same place, where it will soon be claimed by the doe. They are extremely difficult to rear by hand and do not flourish in captivity. Tame bucks become extremely dangerous when they lose their fear of man.

There is considerable mortality of young kids if the weather is cold and wet. Sadly, many get killed or mutilated by grass-cutting machinery. Foxes and loose dogs also account for a number every year. The dog-owning public are remarkably insensitive on this point, often resenting a polite reminder to keep pets under control especially during the time of fawning.

A doe shortly before fawning. *(Photo O Pedersen)*

Twin kids about one week old. *(Photo J Penfold)*

In the south of England kids can be considered as weaned by the middle of August, an event probably hastened by the rut. Farther north does will be found to be in milk well into the start of winter, which should be remembered when considering the starting date for the doe cull. Kids deprived of their mothers while still dependent either fail to survive the winter or may be permanently stunted. Even after weaning, kids continue to learn from the doe until they are turned out the following spring.

Roe have few natural predators in this country except for man. If through neglect of proper management the population is allowed to increase too much, mortality from a combination of starvation and disease will soon become apparent. The heaviest mortality will be in early spring among kids of the previous year. These animals are caught in a downward spiral of debility accelerated by lack of food, pneumonia caused by lung worms and the effects of other parasites such as liver fluke, ticks, keds and lice.

Antlers

Typically a mature roe buck has antlers carrying three points on each: *brow*, *top* and *back point*. They should have prominent *coronets* and the main beams should be well covered with bony outgrowths called *pearling*. They should be between 20 and 30 cm in length (8–12 in).

The whole antler-growing process is hormonally controlled, primarily through the influence of varying daylight hours. The level of the male hormone testosterone declines in the body after the rut, leading eventually to decalcification of a line of bone cells below the coronet, weakening it so that the antler falls off. Some bleeding may occur, but new growth soon laps over the wound

From late winter the antlers grow, covered by velvet. *(Photo J Poutsma)*

Antler growth is completed in late spring, when the velvet dries out and is rubbed off by the buck. *(Photo J Poutsma)*

and elongation proceeds rapidly if there is sufficient protein and other nutrients in the buck's diet. The new growth is covered by *velvet* – a thin layer of tissue containing nerves and blood vessels which make the antlers sensitive and bring building materials to the growing points. A covering of short hairs explains the term. In the spring testosterone levels rise once more, which inhibits further growth and leads to the hardening of the antlers and decay of the velvet. The buck grates his new antlers up and down on convenient tree stems which removes the tatters of velvet and stains the antlers with tree juices until they turn from white or blood-stained to varying shades of brown. Unfortunately it also removes the bark from the tree, which is infuriating to any forester.

A male kid starts to develop

Some bucks never grow more than single spikes and are known as 'Murder Bucks'. *(Photo Sylvan Films)*

A typical six-point mature head with well-marked coronets and fair pearling.

pedicles as small knobs on his forehead by about September. Where the feeding is good, development of the pedicles may be sufficiently advanced by January when the buck is only seven months old for small antlers to develop. These antlers are rarely more than little conical buttons which are cleaned of velvet at the end of January and are shed during the following month. In turn they are replaced by the first true antlers which grow in velvet from February onwards, and should be frayed clean in May or early June. Kid buttons cannot be mistaken for very poor yearling antlers because of the time of the year. Once the regular cycle has become established antlers are shed between October and December, usually the old bucks shed first, and growth of the new set is usually completed by March or April, exceptionally in late February.

Large antlers do not indicate age. Given abundant food during the growing period a young buck of two or three years may grow a

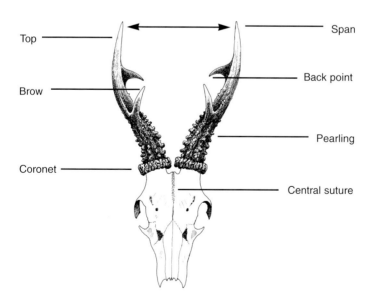

Roe antler terms.

pair of antlers (or *head*) of monumental proportions. Even year-lings have been known to have six-point antlers more than 20 cm (8 in) in length. If food is short in general, or in a particular year, the roe will grow poor antlers, remembering that unlike the larger species growth occurs during the winter when protein-rich food is likely to be in short supply. *The size of antlers grown by a buck can therefore vary enormously from year to year. Contrary to much accepted theory, they are no aid to recognition from one year to another nor of any practical use as a yardstick for selection.* Yearling bucks' antlers are especially misleading. A heavy kid may get a good start in life and grow an unusually promising head. He is, however, the most likely to be ejected early next spring, never to achieve his own territory. Living a hand-to-mouth existence with other non-territorial bucks, he may never grow a good head again. Any buck which succeeds in achieving and holding a territory

benefits from the better feeding and grows bigger antlers, even if his yearling head was very poor.

There is no period of antler improvement in early adult life nor of gradual recession with age, except in the most general terms. Any plan of manage-ment which is based on this widely held but false notion is doomed to failure. However, average antler size in conjunc-tion with average body weights can be used as an index of good or bad management, because both reflect the health of the population and the quality of the environment.

Fraying the velvet later than normal, particularly if it is asso-ciated with delay in shedding the winter coat, should be taken as a signal of possible ill-health, although one caution should be offered: if the weather is mild

There is a local tendency for bucks in the Sussex/Surrey area to grow very narrow heads.

Bucks from the West Country tend to have wider span.

A trophy buck with his cast antler from the previous year. Size may vary from one season to another, but as here the shape may stay constant. *(Photo D Griffith)*

Multi-point antlers, like this buck from Dorset, can result from high feeding or from physiological conditions. *(Photo Udo Geipel)*

when the velvet is ready to fray the buck can remove it in a matter of minutes and it may peel off almost in one piece like a damp glove. If, as often happens in April and May, the weather turns dry and cold, fraying appears to be inhibited and the velvet dries and hardens in place. Bucks with heavily pearled antlers may find it very difficult to remove, though they may be in perfect health. Some years many major bucks will have their antlers half coated with dry velvet well into May.

A perruque buck. Uncontrolled antler growth which never cleans is caused by lack of male hormone. This buck had pea-sized testes. *(Photo Stephen Martin)*

Damage to the pedicles, in this case probably the result of a road accident, will produce a malformed head each year afterwards.

Roe deer seem more liable to accidents than other deer and broken or malformed antlers are by no means uncommon. Wounds to the body or especially damage to the pedicles may mean that a buck produces malformed antlers for the rest of his life. Damage to the antlers themselves, either in velvet or after they have hardened, seldom has an effect beyond the current year. Antlers in velvet are somewhat flexible and a half-fracture during the growing period may result in a bizarre trophy. These are very much valued by some stalkers, especially those from the Continent.

The most fundamental effect on antler growth is, of course, that from a disturbance or interruption of the hormonal balance. If the supply of male hormone is cut off, even temporarily, the antlers may continue to grow but in an uncontrolled way. In the case of a temporary interruption, the antler will eventually harden and probably show exaggerated pearling as a result of its extended growing period. These are known as *mossed heads*. Complete absence of testosterone, for example in the case of castration, will cause the antler to grow continuously and form a mass of tissue on top of the head known as a *perruque* from its wig-like appearance. This mass never hardens or cleans but will eventually become infected and kill the animal. Development in the later stages is very rapid and the perruque may blind the buck by obscuring his eyes before he eventually dies.

The date that a buck's antlers are clean of velvet and, less reliably, the date of casting them give some indication of age. Older bucks tend to fray and to cast earlier than young ones. They are, however, great individualists and this fact should never be disregarded.

Senses

As a beast primarily of thicket and scrub woodland, the roe relies more on his nose and hearing than on eyesight. In our terms, deer see rather indistinctly because of the construction of their eyes. Their ability to make out stationary objects is limited and the image almost monochromatic, like a rather fuzzy black-and-white photograph. To compensate for this they are able to see much better in poor light than we can and are infinitely quicker to detect movement. Roe on the open hill are extremely shy and certainly appear to be able to see very well indeed. It is, however, the movement that they are able to spot rather than the distinctive outline of a man.

A roe's enormous ears can move independently and are always turning this way and that, scanning the area for suspicious noises. If they reacted to every noise deer would be in a perpetual state of

Roe have acute hearing and sense of smell. They are quick to spot movement, but their vision is not sharp.

The head may be moved up and down to catch scent on varying air currents. *(Photo Sylvan Films)*

alarm, but they have a remarkable ability to distinguish between noises which mean danger and others that do not, no matter how loud or distracting. They are aware of deer and other animals moving in the wood, of nearby human activities from shouting to noisy farm machinery, even a nearby picnic party or a forest worker with a chainsaw, and they will apparently take no notice. Crack the smallest twig and they are instantly on the alert.

The structure of a roe's nose, moist, broad and fissured, with wide nostrils and a complex internal structure, shows how important the sense of smell is to a woodland-dwelling creature. The sensitivity of their noses and the world of scent in which they live is a closed book to us, as highly developed and attuned in deer as it is atrophied in humans. Mentally accepting that scent is paramount in their lives is no substitute for living and breathing in that alien world.

Roe are equipped with a variety of scent glands: between the two cleaves of their hooves (*interdigital*); on the hind leg below the hock (*metatarsal*) where there is a small tuft of hair; connected with the urinary tract; and *frontal*, on the forehead between the eyes and the pedicles. Foot scent seems to us a disadvantage because it is fatally attractive to hounds, but is the means whereby a party of roe keeps together in thick cover. Scent from the hock and forehead glands is smeared liberally by the buck round his territory, presumably to indicate his occupancy, and no doubt heavily scented urine has a significance in territory marking although it is not used overtly in rutting behaviour, as is seen in red deer. Roe will often lie in places where wind meets eddy, for example just below the crest of a slope, so that they are protected from two sides. The way of the wind over an area probably has a lot to do with the desirability and boundaries of a buck's territory.

Another sense which is often disregarded is *muscle memory*: that total familiarity with an area which allows a roe to run at full speed along a twisting woodland path without consciously looking for individual obstacles. We benefit from the same sense in our

Glands in the feet leave scent to help group cohesion.

own homes, crossing a room in confidence in the dark and putting out a hand at the right height and the right place for the light switch – unless of course someone has moved the coffee table! Territorial animals derive an enormous advantage from being familiar with their home ground compared with any intruder, and are also better able to escape from predators.

Most disregarded of all is the roe's ability to observe and learn. They are highly successful and adaptable animals, and any stalker who disregards their learning ability is not going to have much consistent success. They are quick to discriminate between the stealthy and purposeful behaviour of the stalker and that of other passers-by. Whether he has a camera or a rifle makes little difference. Forest workers often say how tame the deer are, for they know that this human activity, though noisy, is harmless. I am convinced that every regular visitor to a wood is the subject of minute observation on the part of the deer. No matter how careful the stalker may be to move up or across the wind, the wash of scent spreading downwind from him will have alerted practically every deer in the wood to his presence before the end of his outing. If he stalks the same wood at the same time of day for several successive outings the deer will react by changing their feeding times and will be harder and harder to find. Some of the largest bucks in the record book have been taken by complete beginners who very likely have been doing something so unorthodox through ignorance that a hoary old observer of mankind made one fatal error.

It has long been known that you may not trifle with a deer's nose. So far as the roe buck is concerned, it is equally disastrous to trifle with his powers of observation.

Voice

In a variety of circumstances both sexes bark like a medium-sized dog. Distinguishing male from female purely by their barking is difficult. The challenge or inquisitive bark is a short series of *bow-bow-bow*. At times this will be responded to by other roe in the area so that a chorus starts up which may go on for some minutes. This barking is not, however, so shrill or so persistent as with muntjac. The alarm bark, usually uttered in escape flight can be written as *baaagh-bow-bow-bow*. Challenge barking is more common during the spring when territories are being disputed, and again during the rut.

A variety of other noises are made on occasion, mostly to assist communication. When members of a party become separated and are searching for one another in thick cover they use a muted squeak which is inaudible to human ears at a distance. Kids have a high-pitched squeak to attract the attention of their mothers, and if badly frightened or hurt can scream loudly. During the rut a doe searching for a buck squeaks repeatedly at a slightly lower pitch than the kid. It is rather similar to the noise made by young sparrowhawks. She also squeaks when courting the buck, encouraging him to chase her, and may also produce louder and more agonised noises at particularly hectic moments. These are more fully described in the section on calling (pages 108–110).

In addition to barking more during the rut the buck tends to grumble to himself, and when excited by the prospect of an eligible doe makes a wheezing noise.

Drinking

Roe are rarely seen to drink, except in the hottest weather when they may take a sip from a puddle, or even patronise a cattle trough. Normally they are supposed to get sufficient moisture from the rain and dew. During the summer they are certainly more keen to feed after the dew has started to form. I suspect, however, that when walking through tall wet grass or corn they virtually suck the herbage as they pass and get a good deal of moisture in that way.

Roe are confident swimmers.

Swimming

Considering their narrow hooves, roe are surprisingly bold and powerful swimmers. They have no fear of water and can cross fast currents. Individuals have even been found swimming quite far out in the sea.

Diseases and domestic stock

Farmers are sometimes understandably worried at the possibility of deer acting as a reservoir of diseases which could spread to their stock. Research and experience up to date points to the fact that wild deer are usually healthy and the chance of cross-infection is normally remote. A small number of cases of roe with tuberculosis have been reported, usually from areas where the disease is endemic in the badger population. If concern is expressed by farmers or others about the possibilities of roe being involved in an outbreak of disease, advice should be sought through your local veterinary surgeon to the Game Conservancy or the British Deer Society, from whom specialist advice is obtainable. If on examining a shot deer you notice anything abnormal you must report the fact to the game dealer to whom you sell the carcass, and you can also take it to a veterinary surgeon. If, however, you suspect tuberculosis or any other notifiable disease it must be reported immediately to the Divisional Veterinary Officer (D.V.O.) of the Ministry of Agriculture, Fisheries and Food (M.A.F.F.).

PART 3

Damage

Attitudes to damage

The potential of deer to do damage is the prime reason for having to manage them. The loss which they cause to forestry, agriculture and horticulture is also one of best chances for a keen stalker to get going. Not that shooting deer is the only, or even the best, way of stopping the trouble. There's a lot more to it than that but it is still desperately important to demonstrate to the sufferer that you are willing and able to shoot the marauders. The prime fact is that if you can't get along with the landlord and what he is trying to achieve, you aren't going to manage the deer at all for very long! Second, other activities on the land will almost certainly take precedence over deer stalking so if there are complaints about damage, no matter how trivial they seem to be – do something definite about it as soon as ever possible. Good relations with everyone concerned – farm and forest staff, gamekeeper, land agent, whoever – must be paramount. Achieve that, and then start managing the deer. Otherwise you will get accused, as I have been in the past, of running a private zoo at the landowner's expense.

Deer browsing can seriously check forest crops.

When the fur begins to fly, a prompt display of one or two carcasses says much more than a lecture on selective shooting! So does the offer of a fresh roe liver from time to time.

Because of their preference for browsing highly nutritious young growth, roe like the first shoots of many young plants but rely mainly on the buds, twigs and leaves of trees and shrubs. This does not endear them to the growers of anything from forest trees to suburban shrubs. Bramble is a mainstay of their diet where that useful plant is to be found, though roe find very few growing things really unpalatable, especially when newly planted. It is just an unfortunate coincidence that roses to a deer are merely a particularly scrumptious variety of bramble. In addition, they scrape the bark off small trees when removing the velvet from their antlers in spring and in demonstrations of aggression. Seeing an amenity group of hardwoods wrecked, most of the leading shoots of a young plantation of Norway spruce eaten, or a favourite rose-bed reduced to bare stems instead of a mass of blooms, is understandably infuriating. A heated phone call and an offer of free stalking in exchange for instant results may come your way if your luck is in.

After that, it's up to you to prove your enthusiasm and competence. A stalker's reputation will almost certainly be kept or lost by his ability to keep damage to a reasonable level – in the Forester's opinion, not his own.

Roe fraying has killed this young pine.

Twigs need to be examined closely to determine the culprit. Deer have no upper incisors so the bite is irregular. Rodents bite cleanly.

Identifying Roe Damage

Type of Damage	Cause	Height above Ground	Season
Fraying	Velvet removal Aggressive displays	25 cm – 80 cm	February–May Spring
	Rut		July–Aug
Browsing	Feeding	Up to 1.2 metres	Peaks in winter & spring
Bark stripping	Biting	0.5 – 0.6 metres	(Rarely caused by roe)

Avoiding damage

Excited by the prospect of some longed-for stalking, it is easy to promise more than is really practicable. The dyed-in-the-wool deer-hater's philosophy is 'The only good deer is a dead deer' and he will expect you to haunt the place until all that's left is a pile of bones and empty cartridge cases. First: have you got the time? Can you do a good job here, while not neglecting your other responsibilities? Next, will there be endless replacements waiting in the nearby wood to occupy any vacant space left by your culling and ready to do even worse damage than the late residents? Last, how much damage does he regard as tolerable? Commercial forestry plantations can accept perhaps 5–10 per cent damage provided it is randomly scattered (which is rarely the case). On the other hand, the owner of an orchard or arboretum may quite reasonably demand no damage from deer at all. In that case your work will be in vain and it is better to say straight off, 'You will have to fence' rather than labour mightily and only finish up with a dissatisfied landlord. If he baulks at the expense and orders you to do your best, you can say when the damage goes on, 'I said you'd have to fence'! To exclude roe 95 per cent of the time a fence should be 1.8 m (6 ft) high with meshes not exceeding 15 cm (6 in) square.

The solution to protecting small or specially vulnerable plantations of broadleaved species, oak and cherry especially, which most foresters accept these days is the expensive but effective tree-shelter. Plantations flourish now which would have been impossible to establish without those tombstone-like plastic tubes. The majority of conifers have to be protected with netting sleeves

Recommended Tree Shelter Heights

Largest Deer Species Present	Height Needed
Red	1.8–2 m
Fallow, sika	1.6–1.8 m
Roe, muntjac	1.2 m

rather than solid tubes. Even then there are snags. Not everyone who plants trees is terribly sure what deer species are in the area *and one has to defend the trees against the tallest deer likely to pass that way.* Even though the majority are roe, it is no use putting roe-height tree shelters up if there are occasional fallow. All that happens is that when the tender young leading shoots appear eventually at the top you can be sure that word will pass to any local fallow that there is lettuce for dinner.

They all need good stakes (the taller ones especially), not only to avoid being blown over, but to counter the habit of some deer to lean on them, or to bash them down with their antlers. Some deer also stand on their hind legs to browse the new growth. For these reasons over-enthusiastic weeding should be discouraged, so that the shelters are protected from the deer by a hedge of scrub.

Don't leap to conclusions! This damage is not caused by deer but, looking at the tufts of wool, by sheep.

Preventing fraying damage

Fraying can to some extent be controlled by careful shooting. We know that most fraying is done by young bucks – the majority of it in spring when they are competing for territory. So don't just shoot the first male roe to appear – he is quite likely the major buck who will do a reasonable job of keeping the others out if you leave him in place. In contrast, any yearlings seen in the neighbour-hood of serious fraying damage can be ruthlessly weeded out. One five-acre plantation of three-year Douglas fir yielded a total of seventeen yearlings one spring before the fraying subsided, though admittedly that was in an area of very high roe numbers. The earlier in the open season these yearlings are tackled, the fewer trees they can damage! I have no reservations in culling such animals in April while they are still in velvet if the circumstances make it necessary.

Limiting browsing damage

Trying to limit damage from browsing is really a matter of deer numbers balanced against available food. If, for example, there is little to eat but the trees in a big commercial forest, the population has to be controlled down to a level where damage is reduced *unless the natural food supply can be increased*. Where bramble, willow or other low growth is allowed to colonise along the ride-sides and so on, that will be taken in preference, reducing the pressure on more valuable species and making life easier for the stalker by bringing the deer out where they can be seen and shot.

Tree shelters make it possible to grow trees, even with a high deer density.

Shelters must be the right height for the largest deer species present. These trees have been browsed off by fallow.

Never forget that numbers can only be limited by reducing the breeding herd – that is by culling females.

Lastly, do not assume that damage reported to you has necessarily been done by deer. Very similar damage can be done by rabbits, hares, voles, beetles, squirrels, sheep or goats. Plants may be dying because of poor soil conditions, bad planting or many other reasons. It is all too easy to blame the deer and the stalker – so go and look to make certain!

Protecting farm crops

Unless a farmer is concerned with growing specialist crops, roe deer are less likely to be a source of serious damage than the larger deer. Unfortunately electric fencing is only partially effective against roe, although a well-erected electric fence powered by a high-intensity unit does give some protection at minimum cost, providing the deer are able to see it and that it is placed at such a height that they can investigate it with a damp nose while all four feet are on the ground. So far as roe are concerned this means one wire at a height of 60 cm (2 ft), or three wires at 30, 60 and 90 cm (1, 2 and 3 ft). It is pointless to put an electrified wire above a rabbit fence, for example; the deer will just jump through it. White electrified tape is more effective than ordinary wire and is less likely to get broken.

When a number of deer are feeding in the fields in spring it is worth remembering that almost any agricultural pesticide or fertiliser applied to the field will drive them away – probably until the vulnerable period is over.

In the garden

If there are enthusiastic Bambi-lovers, and that includes most stalkers, there are dedicated Bambi-haters too. In fact a roe buck can do a quicker job of conversion than Billy Graham merely by demolishing one rose bush! Thereby lies the primrose path to getting stalking for many young would-be stalkers who can't afford to rent stalking or go out with a professional. Shooting in the close confines of a garden has, of course, to be done with immense regard for safety and the susceptibilities of neighbours. In many situations it is out of the question.

Roses, with many other flowers and vegetables are liable to attack by roe deer which are not only attracted by their lush richness but quickly recognise that gardens often represent a complete sanctuary to them. Nobody wants to make their home into a prison camp and so traditional fencing is usually out of the question. Some gardens lend themselves to unobtrusive electric fencing which can be switched off during the day. During the winter various proprietary sprays and pastes can be used which can be temporarily effective. In summer care needs to be taken because a spray may harm rapidly growing stems and buds. Unfortunately deer quickly get used to almost anything if they are sufficiently attracted or hungry, so it is wise to use any deterrent only just before the most vulnerable period. In the case of roses this would be at leaf flush and again just before the flower buds break. Human hair, mothballs and, if you have it, lion dung have a similar but even shorter-term deterrent effect. One stalker uses his unwashed socks with great effect! Another leaves a portable radio playing all night.

If you have a dog, one way of reducing the incursions of deer is by use of a buried aerial round the boundary, which works in connection with a radio collar. As the dog nears the buried aerial wire a signal quickly trains it not to cross. In this way the garden can be patrolled from dusk to dawn if he is free to roam at night. One trade name for this device is the *Invisible Fence*.

Problems affecting small woodlands

Roe and pheasants have much the same habitat requirements. They both need low cover, make the greatest use of woodland margins and are found at the highest densities in a typical southern English landscape of scattered copses and small woods with fields in between. While the presence of roe deer may be a potential asset, an uncontrolled population can have a devastating effect on the capacity of a wood to hold pheasants. If all the vegetation has been browsed to a height of 1.2 m (4 ft), which is soon achieved by heavy concentrations of roe, any small wood will become cold and draughty and a disaster from the point of view of the pheasant shooter. Devastation of the ground and shrub layers in this way may be a nature-conservation problem too because of the disappearance of essential food plants for butterflies and cover for ground-nesting birds. The deer themselves will also be affected if their numbers are allowed to build up to this point. A sharply defined browse line should always be taken as a danger sign and an indicator for increased control effort.

The small spinneys and shelter belts which form the backbone of many shoots these days are extremely vulnerable to roe damage, especially in the early years of establishment. Some form of protection will almost certainly be necessary if the spinney is to start to hold pheasants in the shortest possible time. Even if the deer population is reduced to the minimum by control, quite unacceptable damage is still likely, so electric fencing or individual tree protection will almost certainly be necessary if there are roe in the vicinity. There is unlikely to be sufficient space inside such small woods for effective control clearings, although a feed ride can sometimes be made wide enough. When the trees are small the area can be covered by the erection of a high seat. Later the deer will mostly have to be shot in the fields, which means taking advantage of the right crops and the right moment to catch them out there. Narrow belts laid out for a succession of pheasant drives can be gently tapped through in the winter to one or two experienced rifles (see *Moving*, page 107).

PART 4

Management

There is a lot of difference between going out stalking for what you can find and really trying to manage a deer population. Many stalkers do not have the time or opportunity, others call themselves 'deer managers' but are just deer killers. You only begin to become a deer manager when you get more satisfaction from leaving a buck for some good reason than from shooting it.

Deer management in these terms is true conservation, which is defined as the wise use of a renewable natural resource. Every decision taken by the stalker should be related to his plan of management, which must in turn be solidly based on the principles outlined in the box.

A lot of hot air is liberated whenever roe enthusiasts meet, which can be confusing to the beginner. Key words like *rubbish buck*, *Hoffman pyramid*, *sex ratio* and other impressive phrases are thrown around but the higher flights of theory are better left to a later stage. Everyone is an 'expert' as soon as he has shot a roe or two. This 'expert' will claim he knows exactly how many deer he has on his bit of stalking; he can also tell the age of each beast after one glance through the binoculars and he assesses the 'quality' of every buck by the antlers he has grown that year – this one to be kept as an improver, that one to be shot because it will never have a good head. All super stuff, but just as well he does not have to prove it! Once a buck is shot nobody will know if he would have had a better head next year or not. Telling the age of a dead buck, let alone a live one, will only be an estimate to within a year or three. Any bar-room expert will tell you that roe can be counted

---

The Aims of Roe Management

1 Reduce damage

2 Maintain healthy deer in balance with the food and cover available to them

3 Produce a harvest of: (a) venison
                          (b) sport
                          (c) recreation

Careful observation of your ground night and morning is the basis of good management.

accurately; that they grow better heads year by year until they 'go back'; and that it is possible to tell their age. Just remember *'It ain't necessarily so'*! You need some really simple rules to start off with.

Making a plan

Any shooting plan is misleading and unworkable if it assumes that you know precisely how many deer you have, can tell a three-year-old from a five-year-old, or tells you to shoot or spare a buck because of the antlers which he happens to have grown that year. The plan must be based first on the animal's biology, and second on the abilities of a stalker backed by no more than reasonable training and experience.

Three Basic Facts

1   Roe are impossible to count accurately.

2   They are impossible to age accurately in the field.

3   A buck's antlers vary enormously from year to year.

So what can the stalker have as basic rules to guide him on his patch of roe ground? He wants desperately to look after the long-term wellbeing of his deer, protecting the interests of his landowner and getting in return a supply of venison, maybe the odd trophy or two and a good deal of fun. In the end it comes down to some pretty simple questions:

- How many are there about?
- How many should I shoot?
- What sort of bucks?
- What does to cull?

Luckily there are some simple guidelines based on deer biology which will supply some straight answers to these fundamental queries.

How many are there about?

Roe cannot be counted without sophisticated equipment and techniques which are the province of research, not practical management. To give one example, the roe on an area of chalk downland with scattered copses were counted on several occasions by a team of competent field naturalists. They were confident that the population was between twenty-four and thirty-five. An aerial count was then attempted using a helicopter, plus ground observers to prevent movement and recounting, and this was repeated annually for the next six years. The count was never less than 180, and some years exceeded 200. Even then it may have been an underestimate.

If a careful visual count is liable to be so far out, any attempt to add on some percentage for animals unseen is quite meaningless. So forget about trying to count roe accurately – it is a waste of time.

That does not mean that keeping a careful record of the number of deer you see each day is pointless. Quite the reverse. Although an absolute count is impossible, assessing the trend

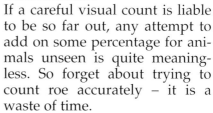

A browse line on ivy gives information on the pressure on available food and by the maximum height, the species responsible.

in numbers from year to year is vital as the only way to judge the impact of your control measures on the population. Some careful counts in late winter and early spring, when the largest number of deer are likely to show up on the fields, can at least give you a minimum figure if you take in as many fields and clearings as possible in a morning. At the same time the proportion of bucks to does should be carefully noted, and also the average number of kids per doe surviving from the previous year. Middle-aged and old bucks will be sufficiently advanced in velvet for some at least to be recognisable, although there will be a tendency for some major bucks to disappear from the fields as soon as there is enough new growth inside the woods to sustain them. Does, already becoming heavy in young, linger on the fields, which may give a false impression of the sex ratio overall.

How many should I shoot?

Deciding how many to shoot on fresh ground can be a problem. Of course you need to be out early and late before the season opens, looking to see what deer you are able to locate, the proportion of males to females and the appearance of every antlered buck so that you can recognise it again. Look, too, at the habitat: is every coppice stool eaten back to the stump? Is every ivy-covered tree bare up to the height of 1 m (3 ft)? That means for sure there are plenty of deer about. If everything is growing unchecked, the betting is they are

Take note of the number of kids per doe in spring – this will affect your cull plans.

thin on the ground. Do you see nothing but does? Somebody has been tanning the bucks and you will have to go easy. Are there other species of deer present? They will all be competing for the same food supplies and the number of roe may be limited.

Roe management is still more of an art than a science. If counting deer is a waste of time, where is one to start? Everybody wants some sort of rule of thumb, at least as a basis for their first attempts at management. Failing any better information, add up the acreage of roe-holding cover on the estate and have a careful look at the habitat, any footmarks (*slots*) and the degree to which any vegetation has been browsed. If the woods are thin and open and the signs of roe not very marked, then a minimum density of one roe to 10 ha (25 acres) or ten per square kilometre might be taken as a guide. If signs of roe are plentiful, and the undergrowth generally thick, then the population is likely to be not less than one roe to 4 ha (10 acres) of cover (twenty-five per square kilometre) and could be very much higher. In ideal habitat healthy populations can be sustained at densities of over one roe to 2 ha (5 acres) or over fifty per square kilometre. Any calculations should, however, be backed up by as much field observation as possible in the spring before the start of the buck season, to try and establish some sort of factual basis. A local poacher may, after all, have done the job for you. From your 'guesstimate' of the total population by observation, calculation or a combination of both, try for a cull of 30 per cent of the estimated number of bucks and 30 per cent of the estimated number of does. So if your population in the spring is thought to number fifty, with twenty bucks of all ages and thirty does, your target for the year might be seven bucks and ten does.

The first shooting plan will probably have more guesswork than fact as its basis. After two or three years of similar spring observations, however, a trend in numbers or a change in sex ratio may start to become apparent. If the population stays the same and is considered excessive, plan to shoot more does.

Roe are a self-regulating species. The spring population is reduced in May by emigration as yearlings of both sexes are chased out of the best places. Your stalking ground may, of course, be some less-good ground and you will suffer an influx of yearlings and will have to increase both the number of yearling bucks to shoot and the proportion of them in the total buck cull. Shooting too many mature bucks will probably result in immigration as vacant territories are filled up. What changes in this case is not the size but the structure of the population, because the incomers will mostly be yearlings with a corresponding increase in damage. As the value and popularity of roe stalking increases, do not assume that a surplus of mature bucks exists over the boundary. Each estate, or group of estates, must be careful these days to preserve their own stock replacements.

Basic Rules for Roe Management

1 Decide how many bucks should be shot

2 Shoot up to that number in these proportions: 60% yearlings
                                                                                     20% middle-aged
                                                                                     20% old

3 Shoot slightly more does than bucks to keep
   the population stable.

What sort of bucks?

Of course a stalker needs to know too what he is allowed to do by law, be aware of what can be done safely in our crowded country-side and have a basic knowledge of the habits of his quarry. Beyond this it isn't asking too much to expect him to be able to identify the deer by species, distinguish between the sexes, and tell the difference between young, middle-aged and old bucks.

Notice that the buck cull is divided up by age class and not by selecting the biggest – or smallest – antlers. Think of yourself as replacing the roe's ancestral predators: wolf and lynx. Many more

A young middle-aged buck. The hindquarters remain comparatively weak until later. *(Photo J Poutsma)*

young would be caught and killed by them than adults – and that is how nature intended things to be. Deer have a comparatively high reproductive rate, fulfilling their role as a prey species. Without predation – theirs or ours – there would be too many deer for their own good, let alone the interests of farmers and foresters. What is vital is that a natural balance should be built into the annual cull. Failing to kill enough females leaves an unnaturally high breeding population, leading to more damage; taking out too many adult bucks gives rise to unwanted turbulence and extra fraying damage, besides spoiling your own chances of a really fine trophy from a full-aged buck once in a while.

Some records may exist of culling levels on your area in the past, otherwise a guess at the population has to be made on the lines suggested above. In the example of a population of fifty roe, twenty male and thirty female, the suggested buck cull of seven bucks should be split into two mature bucks (one old, one middle-aged) and four yearlings. Every effort should be made to exercise the most careful selection, but this selection is in regard to age class; antler size does not come into it.

There are degrees in the intensity of management which is desirable or possible. What one can do on 100 acres of Sussex woodland

Old bucks are the first to clean their antlers in spring, but the last to change coat. *(Photo J Poutsma)*

Young

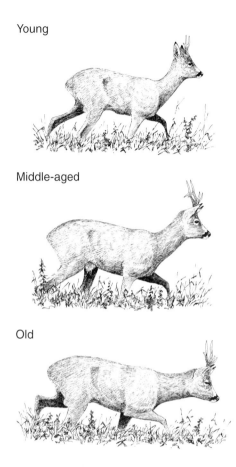

Middle-aged

Old

Roe bucks – build and stance as a guide to age.

is out of the question when faced with 5000 acres of blanket-planted Sitka spruce in the north. If the Sussex stalker only has a handful of deer to shoot in the season, he can afford to be ultra-particular. Even then he should look at the body condition and not the antler growth of his bucks when deciding what to shoot. The activity or apathy of his neighbours will also be very important. By contrast most stalkers in the north are faced with vast woodlands in which deer are difficult to find once the trees are more than five years old, and where the very size of the stalking proposition makes it likely that their efforts will more resemble predation than management. Failing an improvement in forest design, or pending one, one may be forced to take what chances come up. Having to spread your efforts over such a large expanse with few open spaces in which to observe the deer may mean that a particular buck may only be seen once or twice in its lifetime. An effort should, however, be made to get as many of the planned number of yearling bucks as possible and to concentrate on does in their proper season, trying always to finish up with more does than bucks accounted for in the year.

This problem will be a common one in extensive commercial forests until everyone involved in forest planning is finally convinced of the truth that planning provision for efficient deer control is an essential part of good forest practice.

What does to cull?
Although the sex ratio at birth is about even, mortality in the first year is slightly higher among males so more does than bucks must

A family group in early spring. Later most of the young bucks will be driven off.
(Photo R Lowes)

be shot to maintain a level sex ratio, the almost unattainable goal of roe management. In addition, the period of greatest natural mortality is in March, therefore the yearling bucks which are shot in early spring are the survivors of a natural mortality which may account for more than 50 per cent of the total kid crop. On the other hand some doe kids which would otherwise have died the following March will be shot before then, quite properly, as part of the winter cull.

The question will always come up about shooting females which are either pregnant or with a kid at foot. The fact is that all roe does except this year's kids can be assumed to be pregnant, although the developing foetus will be difficult to find until January. Trying to select non-breeders is a waste of time. It is far more important to get the right number of does to keep the population density in balance than to attempt any selection. Kids are weaned before the start of the doe season so they are not dependent for milk on the doe. In Scotland, where the risk of deep snow is greater, a kid may benefit from its mother's presence, but this should not be made an excuse for delaying the cull. There will be that much less food available to the deer if a good part of the doe cull is not achieved before the New Year. One from a pair of twins can be taken if the stalker can spare the time for such finesse. In general terms the doe cull should be split in the proportion of 60 per cent young, 40 per cent mature.

It cannot be repeated too often that population density can only be affected by shooting sufficient does. Yearling does are slightly

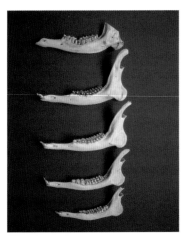

Keep the jaws of roe you shoot, and get help to make a representative collection showing tooth development and wear between youth and age. Note the progressive development of the ridges at the angle of the jaw.

more tolerated by their mothers than yearling bucks are by the males. So there is a tendency for the sex ratio to be biased towards females with a corresponding increase in potential reproductive rate. If a large proportion of bucks is taken, the population will rapidly adjust itself by yearling immigration. Even if there is an overall imbalance and shortage of bucks, roe are not monogamous and every doe will still be pregnant by the end of the rut. Plugging away at the doe cull during the short winter days is demanding, unfashionable and extremely difficult. Straight stalking may have to be supplemented by gentle moves in suitable places, or by getting additional help from local enthusiasts. Everybody wants to go out after a buck in the glorious summer mornings, but only the dedicated will volunteer for does in January. It is regrettable how many stalkers greedily accept more ground than they are really able to manage properly, just for more than their share of trophy bucks.

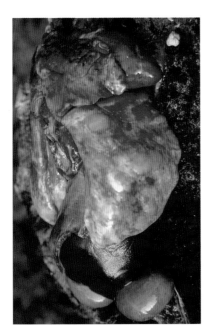

Can you kill the lot?

Those who suffer most from deer damage are on the whole remarkably patient and even tolerant, but the stalker will on occasions find that an owner would like to eliminate deer, at least temporarily, because of the trouble he is suffering. The only way to get rid of deer completely is to clear the area and fence it. Even this expensive action will only have a limited effective span.

Too high a population can lead to losses from parasites. The pale areas on these lungs show the effects of lungworm infestation.

No matter how many deer are shot on an unfenced area some damage is likely to continue, partly because the deer become nocturnal and do the damage when they cannot be seen. Also, for every one that is shot there are usually plenty more waiting to appear. Heavy shooting involves turbulence in the deer population and this in itself may result in worse damage. It is better to attempt to limit the population in the ways which have been suggested, reducing the competition from yearlings but retaining a stable resident herd and taking what other measures for protection may be necessary. Effective management means intelligent collaboration between stalker and forester to produce a scheme of action which has the best chance of success. If trees are planted in such a way as to attract damage those trees will be damaged even if there are only very few deer left in the vicinity. Anything out of the ordinary, ornamental trees in particular, will be sought out and demolished if they are not protected.

Roe as an asset

The third aim of management is to produce a harvest in terms of venison, sport and recreation. No estate can afford to disregard a

The sport of stalking is highly valued. Revenue from visiting stalkers can help to offset costs if they are properly supervised.

constantly regenerating asset. Just marketing the venison which is produced year by year instead of letting it walk away must be good sense. A breeding population of a hundred roe can be expected to produce between thirty and forty carcasses a year, say 450 kg (1000 lb) of venison which commands a ready market.

Marketing the sport should be secondary to maintaining proper control and following a strict scheme of management. The pros and cons of letting are more fully discussed in *Trees and Deer* (published by Swan Hill Press) and *Deer Management in Small Woodlands* published by the Game Conservancy and the British Deer Society. Advice from the Game Conservancy is always advisable before venturing into the often troublesome world of sporting lets. In many cases it is better to find some local enthusiast who for a smaller fee will do a better job throughout the year.

The recreational possibilities other than stalking which roe offer are more extensive than might be imagined. High seats can be let to photographers and on estates where entertaining the public is part of management policy, larger observation platforms can be constructed. At a lower level, the mere presence of deer can enliven a nature trail. Roe are unlikely ever to be a major asset on any estate, but managed properly they do have the potential to be turned from being a pest into a modest source of income.

Records

You've finally shot one! It's a moment every stalker wants to treasure, to store up in his memory bank, a pinnacle of excitement, whether it is a first-ever buck, the successful end to a long stalk, or maybe an especially good or interesting head. Afterwards one wants to share the magic moment with stalker friends or just recall the fine detail of that outing which no matter how thrilling at the time tends to fade and lose its first gloss.

Luckily with roe and muntjac one can usually find some bit of wall (preferably indoors) where a

First-class trophies, like this gold medal head, command a high price from the visitor.

modest collection of nicely cut and boiled-out heads can be exhibited without friction with the rest of the household. The shield, cut and polished or varnished to taste, can be labelled with basic details, with more on the back. Just the sight and feel of those shapely antlers is an enduring satisfaction, but what more can one do? Photographs, if carefully posed and taken in good light are acceptable and can be kept in an album but endless snaps of very obviously dead beasts can only have a clinical interest to the very committed. Too often flash has reflected unnaturally in the eyeballs, or gore is seen oozing or trickling from the corpse. A little care in composing the picture helps to show up the antlers against a neutral background and stop the buck looking altogether too dead. Personally, I disapprove of photos showing the proud hunter posing on or behind a gory heap. We laugh at the Victorian big-game hunter with his boot on the neck of a dead giraffe, and what was tasteless then is inexcusable now. Proudly showing page after page of dead-animal photos is also risky. The glazed look soon develops among your audience even if they happened to have been there at the time, and some casual onlookers might not be in sympathy with Bambi-bashing.

Linking photos with a stalking diary makes a delightful combination to browse in and recall past joys. If you keep notes of weather, time of day and so on, it can even be really useful for reference when you are planning a stalking outing another year, especially from a distance. Small maps can be incorporated which with text and photos can build up a true portrait of some much-

A stalking diary is a pleasant way of recording each outing, but for serious management records are needed which are capable of analysis.

loved piece of ground and the ways of the deer there. But self-discipline is needed to write up each stalk still in the heat of the moment or just as soon as you can afterwards. Otherwise the glitter goes and it becomes just a record of deer shot, which makes the diary dull reading.

Some of us do not have the time or opportunity to try and manage a bit of ground, getting odd days here and there as time or money allow. For those a diary is fine, but anyone who has to report annually to his landowner, or who is really making an attempt at studying the deer and managing them needs figures, not words. Fishing the necessary statistics out of a diary is tedious when all that is needed is a simple analysis sheet. The computer-literate can decide what statistics he will need at the year-end and construct a spreadsheet accordingly which will add itself up or analyse data to order. The last thing most owners or their land agents want is a lyrical description of how busy the stalker has been or how great has been the pleasure of being about in the spring woods . . . and so on. Hard facts, well set out on one sheet of paper are all that busy people need: what has been shot, where and when; what happened to the carcasses and how much money they are owed. The rest can be done, if requested, by a report in person.

For anyone setting out deer management data, these ideas may be useful in their original form or modified to suit individual places. The first is a simple cull record, one sheet per species or you will get in terrible problems.

Cull record

No.	Date	Place	Shot by	Sex	Pregnant? No. of foetuses	Age	Weight	Disposal	Ticket No.

At the end of the season this form will have all the basic information available you need for a summary, including that valuable statistic for assessing condition, average weight.

A year-end summary is what most owners want to see from their stalkers, i.e. what you said you were going to do, and whether you did it. It is easy as that.

For your own purposes of good deer management these two will show most of what you need from one year to another. You may also do a spring count each year, and while it may not bear much relation to the actual numbers of deer present, it will show a useful

Year-end summary

Planned cull				Actual cull				Total males culled	Total females culled
♂ M	♂ Y	♀	T	♂ M	♂ Y	♀	T		

(M = mature, Y = young, T = total)

trend if you do it the same way each year. It should be recorded in the same way.

If, as deer manager, you are letting stalking, then a record of trophies shot is vital. Each client takes his trophies off with him, so without records there will be nothing to show any new clients what care is going into management, and what trophy quality he can expect. That is where details of antler measurements, the estimated age of each buck shot, the skull weight and, if available, the C.I.C. score of any medal-class heads need to be shown against photos of noteworthy bucks and – preferably separate – snaps of happy, contented clients.

Trophy record

No.	Date	Place	Shot by	Age	Pts	Length	Trophy wt	Remarks

If you don't keep some records like these, especially the first two, and learn from them, then you aren't managing your deer, you are just exploiting them.

PART 5

Stalking Know-how

Legal considerations

The law is very strict on the possession and use of firearms. Through anti-sport propaganda and media hype the public are also apprehensive at the sight of anyone carrying a rifle, so on both counts every stalker has to be ultra-particular to obey the law and act responsibly at all times. There will be times when a slight bending of the rules seems reasonable, but do not be tempted – the future depends on every field sportsman behaving immaculately at all times.

Firearm Certificate
A police Firearm Certificate (F.A.C.) is needed before you may own or use a rifle in Britain. You must have it with you when you go out stalking. There are age restrictions and applicants have to show that they have somewhere suitable to use the weapon. A visitor to Britain must possess a Visitor's Permit, applied for by his shooting host prior to the visit. Under certain conditions a rifle may be used by a non-certificate holder provided the licence-holder for that rifle (or his servant, such as a gamekeeper) is present. *Firearms Act 1968 as amended.*

Licence to kill game
A Game Licence (bought from post offices) is needed for deer stalking. They run from 1 August to 31 July. However, a licence is not required to shoot deer on enclosed land. *Game Licences Act 1860.* The Home Office has for some time indicated it as their intention to abolish Game Licences but they have not yet done so.

Sale of venison
You can only sell venison to a licensed Game Dealer in England and Wales or a licenced venison dealer in Scotland. *Deer Act 1991; Deer (Scotland) Act 1996.*

Firearms permitted for killing deer in the United Kingdom
The law in this respect varies between England and Wales,

Scotland and Northern Ireland. What may be legal in one country may be illegal in another, and restrictions may vary between species, so care is needed in the choice of a rifle so that you can stalk throughout Britain without problems. It should be noted that bowhunting for deer is not legal anywhere in Britain.

In **England and Wales**, a rifle is illegal for use to kill deer if it has a calibre of less than .240 in or a muzzle energy of less than 2305 joules (1700 ft/lb). To comply a rifle must exceed both these criteria. Bullets must be soft- or hollow-nosed.

It is illegal to use a shotgun against deer. The only exceptions to this rule are: first that a shotgun may be used for the purpose of preventing the suffering of an injured or diseased deer (*Deer Act 1991, section 6*); and secondly where an individual is authorised to do so under the *Deer Act 1991, section 7* to prevent serious damage to crops or growing timber. The shotgun used in the second case (but not the first) must be not less than 12-bore with a cartridge containing shot each of which is .203 in (5.16 mm), that is to say AAA, or loaded with a single non-spherical projectile weighing not less than 350 grains (22.68 g).

In **Scotland** there is no minimum calibre of rifle specified, but restrictions are placed on the ammunition used.

	Bullet Weight Grains (Grams)		Muzzle Velocity Ft/sec (M/sec)		Muzzle Energy Ft/lb (Joules)	
Any species of deer	100	(6.48)	2450	(746.76)	1750	(2373)
Roe deer only	50	(3.24)	2450	(746.76)	1000	(1356)

In practical terms this means that the minimum calibre/load for roe in Scotland is the .222 Remington, but the .243 Winchester (100-grain bullet) is the minimum which is legal in England and for all deer in Scotland. Some well-tried cartridges, such as the .256 (6.5×54) Mannlicher, the .30-30 Winchester and even some heavy-bullet loads for otherwise legal rounds, e.g. 220 grain for the .30-06, are outlawed by Scottish legislation because of their low muzzle velocity.

As in England and Wales, a shotgun can only be used to prevent serious damage to crops by authorised persons. The shotgun must be 12-bore minimum but the specified ammunition varies:

- For all species of deer, either a single non-spherical bullet of not less than 380 grains (24.62 g) or pellets of size not less than SSG
- For roe deer only, pellets of size not less than AAA

The Deer (Firearms etc.) (Scotland) Order 1985

Roe deer do not occur in **Northern Ireland**, but for reference the regulations are as follows:

- Rifle: Minimum calibre .236 in
- Shotgun: A shotgun can only be used against deer for the protection of growing crops and timber. It must be not less than 12-bore loaded with either a single non-spherical bullet of not less than 350 grains (22.68 g) or pellets of not less than AAA

The Wildlife (Northern Ireland) Order 1985

Careful note should be taken of these provisions, particularly the fact that the shotgun is effectively banned throughout the country. Stalkers who intend to travel for their sport should choose a rifle

---

The Safety Code

1   Treat every rifle as if it were loaded.
2.   Never have a cartridge in the chamber or the magazine, except when actually stalking.
3.   Never point a rifle at any unidentified object or use the scope sight instead of binoculars.
4.   Always check that a rifle is unloaded before climbing into a high seat, negotiating a fence or other obstacle, entering a vehicle or house, and when putting it in a case or cover. Lock it away from thieves and children. Store the bolt and ammunition separately from the rifle.
5.   Be familiar with the mechanism before use, especially trigger pull, safety catch and magazine. Do not tamper with them.
6.   Keep the barrel clean, free from oil, mud, snow or any obstruction. Check after a fall.
7.   Use the safety catch but do not trust it.
8.   Loading and unloading are moments of special danger. Where is your muzzle pointing?
9.   Have the rifle checked periodically by a competent rifle-smith.
10.   Remember that a rifle bullet is lethal at several thousand metres. Earth is the only safe backstop; woods are not. Never fire over or near a skyline.
11.   Do not carry the rifle slung horizontally, or in any way that it can menace others.
12.   Familiarise yourself with your stalking ground and especially any footpaths, official or otherwise. Get to know the keeper and the farm and woodland staff. Ask them about their work and movements and tell them about yours.
13.   Do not mix stalking and drinking.

---

which complies with the differing requirements north and south of the Scottish border. All .22 rifles, regardless of the ballistics of the cartridge, are at present illegal in England and Wales for use against deer, while in Scotland roe may be shot with the more potent .22 centrefires from .222 Remington upwards. It is illogical, but the law as it stands must be obeyed.

Misunderstandings have arisen on the English side of the border regarding the use of .22 rifles which have a muzzle energy in excess of 1700 ft/lb. A rifle must comply with the requirements for calibre as well as muzzle energy to be legal for deer in England and Wales. It is, however, the calibre of the rifle barrel, not the bullet, which is the determining factor and therefore sabot cartridges such as the Remington Accelerator in .308 etc. do comply with the law, although effectively a .22 bullet is discharged. Unfortunately these rounds do not seem as accurate as traditional loadings.

In addition to the prohibitions mentioned in the table, all other methods of taking or killing deer, or attempting to kill them, are illegal. Deer may not be trapped or snared, nor shot at with any type of arrow or other missile. Wounded deer may not be killed with sub-legal rifles even in the event of a traffic incident. A shotgun (unspecified) may be used.

Shooting from vehicles
It is illegal to shoot deer from a vehicle except in a deer park.

Safety and security
Safety has to be paramount at all times, no matter how brief the chance at a longed-for trophy, or how great the pressure to shoot more deer.

Every effort must be made to avoid rifles or ammunition falling into the hands of criminals or children. Traditional care is not enough these days. Cars and houses are constantly being broken into and each instance of carelessness, or even bad luck, will be used by the authorities to press for further restrictions on legitimate firearms users. A strong steel cabinet is now essential. The bolt and ammunition should be in a separate locked compartment.

It is advisable never to leave a rifle, shotgun or ammunition in an unattended car, as loss will probably result in action by the police. The bolt and ammunition should always be kept separate from the weapon. The bolt is an awkward thing to put in your pocket. Recently a handy *bolt holster* has been marketed by Spencer Research Ltd of Bath. It has a belt loop and a sheath of heavy-duty synthetic material.

The law insists that when you have your rifle with you, you must also be able to produce your Firearm Certificate.

Insurance

You need to have insurance, not only against claims for any damage you may do, but for the stalking equipment you build up. Third-party claims are best covered by membership of either B.D.S. or B.A.S.C. Membership of B.A.S.C., for example gives cover to members for 'legal liability for bodily injury and damage to property up to £5,000,000 resulting from shooting or conservation activity'. B.D.S. cover is similar. Any professional activity needs separate cover. Some householders' comprehensive policies, Hiscocks for example, specifically cover sporting guns and equipment.

Close seasons

Close seasons are given in the table below. The relevant Acts are:

- *The Deer Act 1991*
- *The Deer (Scotland) Act 1996*
- *The Wildlife (Northern Ireland) Order 1985*

Statutory Close Seasons

Species	Sex	England & Wales	Scotland	Northern Ireland
Red	Stags	1 May – 31 July	21 October – 30 June	1 May – 31 July
	Hinds	1 March – 31 October	16 February – 20 October	1 March – 31 October
Red/Sika Hybrids	Stags		21 October – 30 June	
	Hinds		16 February – 20 October	
Sika	Stags	1 May – 31 July	21 October – 30 June	1 May – 31 July
	Hinds	1 March – 31 October	16 February – 20 October	1 March – 31 October
Fallow	Bucks	1 May – 31 July	1 May – 31 July	1 May – 31 July
	Does	1 March – 31 October	16 February – 20 October	1 March – 31 October
Roe	Bucks	1 November – 31 March	21 October – 31 March	
	Does	1 March – 31 October	1 April – 20 October	

There is no legal close season for muntjac or Chinese water deer. However, these species do come within the legislation regarding the use of rifles for killing deer.

There are those who argue that the open seasons are too long, and others that they are too short. Those who find them too long should be reminded that nobody is forced to shoot a roe buck on 1 April, or to continue shooting does until they are heavily pregnant. If the stalker is not hard pressed to achieve the right number of each sex, he can afford to be more discriminating. If on the other hand you find the seasons too short because of the need to get more deer, and you are tempted to shoot them out of season, then the truth is either that you have not put enough effort into getting the right number during the season, or that under the circumstances the target set is too great for the ability of the man. Efficiency can be improved by better training and often by better co-operation with the forester and his staff. A professional stalker faced with an enormous area to cover may be able to recruit reliable amateur help. A part-timer may have over-estimated the amount of time which he can spare for his hobby. Circumstances too can change. You are being greedy if you have more than you can deal with properly and are abusing the deer that you have the privilege of managing. Share it with another enthusiast.

Merely hounding deer throughout the year, in season and out, is self-defeating. The deer become increasingly shy, and damage within the plantations may even increase because they do not dare to go into the open to feed. Above all public opinion, which is tender-hearted towards deer, will surely react if deer are consistently mistreated, no matter what let-out clauses in the law may be invoked by the perpetrators.

Night shooting

It is an offence to take or wilfully kill deer between one hour after sunset and one hour before sunrise. There are some specific exceptions for the protection of crops which are outside the scope of this book. In Scotland night shooting is controlled by the Deer Commission Scotland (*Deer Act (Scotland) 1996, section 18*).

Rifles

What sort of rifle?

Ask almost any professional stalker what he uses, and it will be a bolt action, with a magazine under the bolt holding four or five cartridges. He wants a totally reliable tool, and so do you. Such weapons are comparatively cheap to make, but have excellent

The roe stalker goes solo, so his gear must be light and well chosen.

potential for accuracy. Weights vary, from super-lightweights to heavy-barrel jobs more suitable for target shooting. Don't go to either extreme until you have more experience. Heavy weight means more for you to carry – light weight equals heavy recoil. Remember, too, that a very short barrel may look handy, but the muzzle-blast can be very off-putting and can start a flinch as easily as heavy recoil. Muzzle brakes have the same snag.

You will be fitting a scope sight, so look to see if the rifle is fitted with mounting blocks, or pre-drilled holes where these can be fitted. The comb of the stock should be high enough so that when the rifle is mounted to your shoulder there should be a comfortable contact with the side of your face and with your eye lined up with the scope. Many manufacturers now offer plastic stocks in place of the traditional walnut. While they are not as ornamental, plastic stocks are not liable to warp due to variations in humidity and so have a great deal to commend them.

Some magazines are removable boxes, but most are fixed in place. If the bottom plate swings downwards the cartridges in the magazine can be quickly taken out; otherwise the bolt has to be worked to and fro to extract each one, which is tedious. The

Careful zeroing gives confidence in your rifle. Here I am using a Parker-Hale in .30-06 fitted with a Harris bipod. The scope is 4×40 by Pecar.

Sauer 202 bolt-action rifle fitted with a Zeiss vari-power scope on Apel swing mounts.

bottom plate must fit snugly, not clicking when inadvertently pressed, and the safety catch should be positive; not easily jarred or brushed off, but silent in operation. I have seen many deer alarmed by that fatal click.

The trigger must have a clean pull-off, without creeping, and neither heavy nor too light – about 1.6 kg (3½ lb) suits most people. Some single-barrelled rifles are fitted with two triggers, which may be confusing. This is a hair-trigger mechanism and unsuitable for a beginner.

New or second-hand? There are bargains to be picked up in second-hand rifles which will often have a scope sight already attached. Do not, however, be tempted by a rifle merely because it is cheap. It may have a barrel which is neglected or worn out by years of professional use, have some fault in the bedding which makes it unreliable and is the reason for its being sold, or be chambered for a cartridge which is difficult to obtain or unsuitable for roe. The scope, too, may be fogged, scratched, or have a loose lens, which is fatal to accuracy. Find, if you can, a real riflesmith and take his advice.

What calibre?

The choice of calibre needs thought, although the needs of the roe stalker are neither so limited nor so precise as many enthusiasts will claim. It is wise to choose a modern calibre in general use so

that the ammunition can be easily bought, one for which a variety of loads are available and, for the single-rifle stalker, one which is equally suitable for the larger deer which he may eventually hope to shoot.

A take-down rifle is extremely convenient for travelling. The Blaser rifle not only can be taken to pieces but has interchangeable barrels for different calibres.

Another view of the Blaser rifle assembled with its straight-pull bolt.

Because of the different legal requirements in Scotland the specialist roe stalker north of the border, who possibly may have a heavier rifle for other species, has a choice of .22 centre-fire calibres which are ideal for roe. These are shown in the box.

Popular Rifle Calibres Legal for All Deer in the UK	
Calibre	Name
.243	Winchester (100 grain bullet)
.270	Winchester
.275 (7 mm×57)	Rigby
.30-06	Springfield
.308	Winchester
6.5 mm×55	

Ballistic details for all these cartridges will be found in Appendix 2.

Popular Rifle Calibres Legal for Roe Only in Scotland	
Calibre	Name
.243	Winchester (100 grain bullet)
.222	Remington
.223	Remington
.22-250	Remington

What ammunition?

For most of the cartridges listed there will be suitable and unsuitable bullets for roe. Choosing the right bullet is much more important than selecting one calibre or another. Only expanding bullets are legal for deer, but these can be soft-point or hollow- nose. Ballistic-nylon-tipped bullets are designed to expand. 'Solid' (non-expanding) bullets are only suitable for target shooting or for elephants etc. Roe are small animals with light bones. A bullet designed for deep penetration and slow expansion suitable for heavier game, will often slip through the ribcage of a roe and exit, retaining much of its energy instead of expending it with lethal effect in the tissues. Very lightly constructed bullets have been developed for the transatlantic sport of long-range varminting on targets up to the size of foxes. These expand too quickly on roe, especially if they encounter a bone on entry, creating great damage to the meat and, at worst, failing to penetrate deeply enough to be fatal. Every bullet is therefore a compromise so that it will behave more or less in the same manner regardless of the range, or whether it gets a hard or soft passage through the target animal. Contrary to widespread belief, within the same calibre large bullets do less damage; lightweight bullets do more.

Factory ammunition is the safest option for beginners. It is, however, usually loaded to the maximum and changes may be made without warning in specifications both as to load and to bullet characteristics from batch to batch. Buy reasonably large batches at a time to ensure uniformity and always check performance of a new lot with a zeroing session (see page 81). Hand-loaders, providing they experiment as far as possible on the range and not

---

Recommended Bullet Weights for Roe
The following list is offered as no more than as a suggestion and a starting point:

Calibre & name	Bullet weights
.243 Winchester	100, 105 grains
.270 Winchester	130 grains
.275 Rigby (7 mm×57)	140 grains
.30-06 Springfield	130, 150 grains
.308 Winchester	150 grains
6.5 mm×55	139 grains

---

on deer, have a world of choice at their feet in working up the most suitable load within the legal requirements. This can be a hobby on its own, but expert tuition is essential.

Sights and accessories

Forget about any other sort of sights: open, aperture, fancy electronic dot or whatever. For woodland stalking you need the best-quality scope sight your budget can run to. It must be attached to the rifle with mounts which never shift, and these alone can be expensive, so allocate a large chunk of what you can afford to a good scope. The rifle underneath, believe it or not, is less important!

All scopes are designed with an *eye relief* of about 7.5 cm (3 in), i.e. a full sight picture is obtained when the eye is about this distance from the eyepiece. If the scope is mounted too far forward on the rifle it will be necessary to crane the head forwards uncomfortably. If it is too far back the stalker will be rewarded by a painful injury to his eyebrow when the rifle recoils. Usually this happens when trying a prone shot uphill. Some scopes are fitted with a neoprene ring on the eyepiece to minimise the trouble, but even so the stalker is liable to flinch and it is much better to make sure that the

The range of Zeiss ZM/Z Riflescopes. Quality is more important with scopes than with the rifle itself.

A Zeiss Diavari Z 1.5-6×42, one of the most practical and versatile scopes. It is mounted on a Brenneke rifle with Apel mounts.

scope is mounted properly in the first place.

Cheap scopes made primarily for .22 rifles are unlikely to be suitable for two reasons: they will not be designed for the heavy recoil of a deer rifle, which may unship the interior lenses to say nothing of giving you a biff on the eyebrow because the eye relief may be too short. The light-gathering power may also be insufficient for woodland stalking conditions. Some budget-priced scopes give years of satisfactory service, though the odd one can give trouble. The care which is lavished on more expensive scopes in grinding and coating the lenses and in sound construction does pay off in utter reliability, brilliance, clarity and superior light transmission.

Scopes have to be waterproof. The least trace of moisture entering the tube will fog the lens. This mist appears and disappears in a maddening way according to the temperature. In the unlikely event of fogging, an expensive scope should be sent back to the

Zeiss reticles

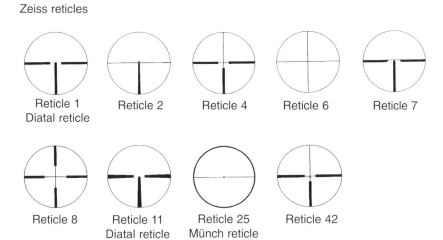

Scope reticles. Nos. 1 and 4 are probably the best for woodland stalking.

makers. A cheap one is better thrown away. Never attempt to dismantle a scope sight for any reason.

The aiming mark or reticle needs to be fairly definite for shooting in poor light. Traditional crosshairs can vanish when, for example, one is faced with a shot late at night in deep shade. Some stalkers like a flat-topped post, intercepted by a horizontal line to avoid canting. Others favour a combination reticle which has three or four thick outer posts extended into the centre of the picture by fine lines. This has the advantage of a precise aiming point for good light, backed up by thick posts if a wounded animal has to be taken when very little light remains. A post reticle with a fine point tends to make one shoot progressively higher as the light goes because the tip of the post cannot be seen. Various illuminated reticles are also available, but one should remember that deer shooting legally stops one hour after sunset until one hour before sunrise, and at these times a normal reticle can easily be seen. It is also necessary to see the target as well as the reticle, and the use of artificial light for deer shooting is equally forbidden. Illuminated reticles can also temporarily upset the stalker's twilight vision.

Long shots are not the rule in roe stalking. In thick woodland any deer that is seen is likely to be well within range, and even on open ground the stalker should restrict himself to shots within a maximum of 150 m (160 yd). The vital areas on a roe are small enough at this range, even in the rare event of a steady shooting position being possible. For this reason high magnification is unnecessary, six-power (6×) being fashionable nowadays, although my preference is 4× for woodland work. Variable-power scopes seem attractive on paper but compared with fixed-power instruments they are heavier, and there is more to go wrong. With some models the length of the rear bell is so great that the scope cannot be satisfactorily mounted on many rifles.

Like binoculars, scopes are given two measurements, the magnification and the size of the object lens (the one farthest from your eye). Divide one by the other to get the *exit pupil* diameter, e.g. 4×32: exit pupil = 8 mm. The human eye is only capable of expanding to about 7 mm in poor light, so a

A fixed-power scope is a reliable friend. This 6× model is mounted on a shotgun-type single-shot rifle.

High magnification and a large object lens oblige the scope to be mounted high above the barrel, which can make the rifle awkward to shoot.

scope (or binoculars) with an exit pupil diameter of 7 or more will let more light through that the eye can accept. Much smaller than that and you will not be able to see as much in poor light through the scope as you can with the naked eye.

So much is straightforward, but you will also come across the term *twilight performance* which is calculated by this formula:

Twilight factor = square root of (magnification $\times$ object lens diameter)
e.g. 4×40 = twilight factor of 12.6; 8×40 = twilight factor of 17.8. That is, that the larger figure indicates better performance in poor light.

High magnification seems to score better, but high power usually means a poor field of view and critical focus. To keep the exit pupil figure up, the lenses, and so the whole scope, may have to be very large and heavy. In addition any shake is magnified that much more, which tends to cancel out the benefit. So as usual, one has to compromise. An object lens of about 40 mm is a good compromise; much less than this reduces the amount of light passing through the instrument, much more and you have a very bulky sight that has to be mounted high above the barrel. This makes good contact between cheek and stock difficult, even with rifles which have a high comb especially for the purpose. It is also very easy to cant the rifle, another factor in loss of accuracy especially at longer ranges. One is not shooting at night. In fact it is bad practice to take a shot at last light – too much can go wrong and the flash blinds you for minutes afterwards. For wild boar or similar night work from a steady rest such as a high seat, higher power and larger lenses may be appropriate.

When matching the scope to its mounts, take careful note of the central tube diameter. Some are 25.4 mm (1 in), others are 30 mm (1.18 in). It is possible to distort the tube by trying to fit the wrong size of mount.

For woodland stalking a pair of scope caps is needed because the rifle is carried ready for use, unlike the more deliberate business of red deer stalking on the open hill, where it is protected by a cover until the last stages of a stalk. Some scope caps have plastic pieces to cover the lenses so that one can see through them. Inevitably the light transmission and general clarity is rather poor. It is better to use the flip-up type which can be released at the last moment in wet weather.

Slings

Because the rifle always needs to be ready for use and the stalker has to use his binoculars all the time, he carries his rifle slung on one shoulder (see page 94). The two essentials are that it should not slip and that it should not rattle. It is best to buy a sling of the right length without an adjusting buckle and to attach it to the rifle with a thong rather than the usual brass button, which is not only noisy but can damage the woodwork. The sling swivels on the rifle must not rattle either. Nothing is more alarming to deer than a metallic noise. Some slings are lined with felt or rubber to prevent them slipping off the shoulder. A saddler will produce a sling for you made out of a leather rein covered with a non-slip rubber sleeve.

Modern sporting rifles are not usually designed to take the sideways stresses involved when one adopts the target-shooter's technique of using the sling as an additional arm support. Erratic shooting results from straining the woodwork into contact with the barrel and interfering with

A good non-rattle, non-slip sling made by Steve Wright of Huntly.

its natural vibrations. In any case the chances of taking a deliberate prone shot at a roe are fairly remote, not to speak of the contortions necessary to get the sling braced round one's upper arm while a buck looks on.

Rifle maintenance

Although rifle cartridges leave a non-corrosive residue, this does not protect the barrel from rust. Deposits also build up in the angle between the grooves and the lands of the rifling, and will eventually have a serious effect on accuracy. As a matter of routine after a stalking expedition the barrel should be mopped out using a flannelette patch on a jag designed for the calibre. The patch should be moistened with a nitro solvent and rust preventer, such as Parker-Hale 009, successive patches being used until they come out clean. Before the next outing a clean dry patch should be put through the bore in order to remove any trace of oil. Even a small amount of oil can affect the accuracy of the first shot; an excessive amount can even increase pressures to a dangerous level.

More intensive cleaning should be carried out periodically. Swab the inside of the barrel using a patch saturated with 009, which will probably emerge with a greenish stain caused by metal from the bullet jackets. If it does, a phosphor-bronze brush should be dipped in the solvent and worked briskly up and down the bore before repeating the patch treatment. This will take out accumulated residues. After treatment the barrel should be oiled in the usual way. If there was a significant amount of fouling some alteration in zero may be apparent after cleaning, so carry out the treatment just before a zeroing session, not only to check that the rifle is 'on', but to restore it to its normal condition. Stalking

---

Cleaning Equipment
_____

Cleaning rod
Brass jag to suit bore
Phosphor-bronze brush to suit bore
Nitro-powder solvent (e.g. Parker-Hale 009)
Lubricant and water repellent (e.g. WD-40)
Flannelette patches
Old toothbrush
Turnscrews ground to fit the tang and recoil stop pins
Allen keys or turnscrews to fit the scope mounts
Cotton rags

---

differs completely from target shooting because the first shot is the vital one. There is rarely an opportunity to try a rifle before the start of a woodland stalking expedition.

The bolt should, of course be removed at the end of each stalk and stored separately from the rifle. It must be carefully but lightly oiled, using an old toothbrush to clean out its many corners. Likewise the bolt lug recesses and the magazine need brushing out and oiling. The exterior steel work should be wiped over with an oily cloth every time the rifle is handled; even finger marks can start corrosion! Any splash of blood can only be removed with a damp cloth before oiling. If the barrel is free-floating or relieved, that is to say not in contact with the woodwork throughout its length, a piece of paper should be slipped underneath it to check that there is no dirt in the gap or an unexpected point of contact with the stock. Intermittent contact between metal and woodwork interferes with the natural vibrations of the rifle barrel when it is fired, resulting in a serious loss of accuracy.

Particular care must always be taken on this point whenever the action is taken out of the woodwork for any reason, such as altering the trigger pull. A trial with a piece of paper and a check of zero is always advisable. Do not have too many shots at one session. Bedding problems often show themselves by a tendency for the group to climb as the barrel heats up after a few quick shots. Otherwise there may be just a general loss of accuracy. The stalker is always most concerned about the accuracy of his first shot from a cold barrel. There are no sighting shots in deer stalking.

Keep all screws tight. It is a good routine before checking for zero to test the tightness of the tang and recoil stop screws, the screws holding the scope mounting blocks to the action, the tightening screws of the scope mounts, and the small scope ring screws. All screws on a new rifle take time to bed in, and may keep needing to be tightened after every few shots. A set of properly ground gunmakers' turnscrews is necessary for this, otherwise the screw slots will become burred and unsightly.

Setting the weight of trigger pull largely depends on the sensitivity of the shooter's finger. Most rifles are sent out from the factory with a very heavy pull, presumably for reasons of safety, but a heavy pull makes accurate shooting, especially in the off-hand position, extremely difficult. Most stalkers find a crisp pull of around 1.6 kg (3½ lb) a good compromise, while others prefer a light pull of about 1.2 kg (2¾ lb). The majority like a single pull with no perceptible movement before the rifle fires, but some with army experience are used to a two-stage trigger, taking up an initial pressure or slack before actually firing. Unless you know precisely what you are doing and have the instruction sheet for your rifle, adjusting the trigger pull for weight, creep or backlash should be left to an experienced riflesmith.

Zeroing

No matter how careful you are, a rifle will be subject to changes in temperature and humidity. It will suffer the odd knock or fall. Even placing the rifle flat on a car seat with a pile of coats on top sets up stresses in the barrel which we often forget about. The result of one or all of these is a gradual or even a dramatic change in the point of impact of the bullet, which needs to be corrected first by checking if anything mechanical is wrong, and second by altering the sights. The process is called *zeroing*.

Before attempting to alter the sights, all screws should be checked for tightness, and barrels which are relieved or free-floating from the woodwork should be checked for the presence of dirt or unplanned points of contact with the woodwork due to warping. The rifle should be given a thorough clean and a safe place should be chosen where a number of shots can be taken in comfort and safety without disturbing other people. Ensure that your Firearm Certificate permits zeroing on your chosen piece of land.

A glance at the trajectory diagram (page 82) will show that the bullet cuts the line of sight at two places, first at about 20 m (60 ft)

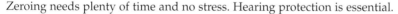

Zeroing needs plenty of time and no stress. Hearing protection is essential.

A good solid bench rest and safe shooting in a cutting make for good zeroing. *(Photo D Griffith)*

and then at the range selected. Gross adjustments should be done at the shorter range, besides anything to make sure that in the event of serious misalignment the bullet still hits the paper and the backstop.

A rough check can be made by placing the rifle with the bolt removed on a firm bench where it can be aligned with the target by looking down the barrel. Without moving the rifle a glance through the scope sight will show whether it is roughly on target or not. This is called *bore sighting*. Removing the protective caps from the adjustment turrets on the scope, corrections are made to the setting so that the picture through the sight and through the

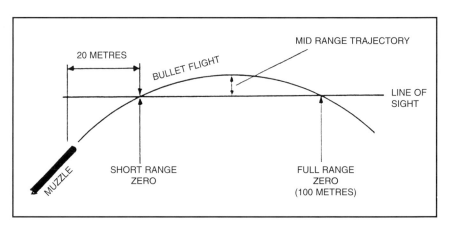

Trajectory diagram. The bullet crosses the line of sight in two places because of the height of the scope sight above the bore. Rough zeroing can be done at the short range point of intersection, which will be at about 20 metres. Final adjustments can then be made at the full range.

bore coincide. Replace the bolt and take one careful shot at 20 m (60 ft). The rifle should then be clamped with the scope reticle centred on the target bull, and without moving it, the vertical and lateral adjustments should be used *to bring the reticle to the shot hole*. A second shot will then confirm whether these adjustments have been made accurately. After this one can zero the rifle at any selected range with a reasonable expectation of hitting the target with the first shot. To allow for individual variation between shots at full range, a group of three should always be made before altering the sights. Give yourself plenty of time for a zeroing session, otherwise the task will be skimped and you will have no confidence in the rifle afterwards.

Because roe are small targets and are usually shot at comparatively short range, the rifle should be zeroed so that the bullet is never far from the line of sight between the muzzle and 150 m. Reference to the ballistic table in Appendix 2 will give the zeroing range and the maximum error for most cartridges in common use. A hundred yards (92 m) is the recognised zeroing distance for roe stalking.

In addition to checking the sights periodically, and at any time after a period of disuse, or when the last shot seemed to go slightly wrong, a zeroing session should be the opportunity for practice. Most stalkers shoot comparatively few roe in the year, and this does not give enough familiarity with the rifle to maintain a sufficiently high standard. Regular range practice is the answer. In addition to shooting prone the opportunity should be taken to practise kneeling, sitting and standing shots making the best advantage of trees and fence posts and becoming familiar with the use of a stalking stick to improve one's accuracy. For any range work everyone present should wear ear muffs to protect their hearing.

The collimator
Scope-sighted rifles are notorious for getting out of adjustment, although it is more likely to be the fault of the rifle or the mounts rather than the scope itself. Whatever the cause, stalkers do need to check the zero from time to time, and taking a shot or two is not always convenient. The collimator is a very handy device for this purpose, or for getting a preliminary rough zero when fitting a new scope before going on to careful sighting-in.

The instrument itself is a short tube with a number of mandrels which allow it to be fitted into the muzzle of most common deer rifles. It is essential to have one of precisely the correct diameter to make a good fit in the bore. Looking through the scope one sees a grid, each square representing 1 in at 100 yd. If the scope reticle coincides with the centre of the grid, it is more or less zeroed – well

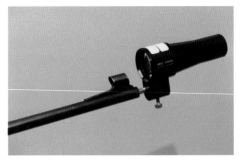

Nikko Sterling Collimator for checking zero. Notes should be made of the setting for each load.

enough to make a starting point for sighting-in first at 20 yd and then at 100. It is not exact because of varia- tions in the height of the scope, vibrations of the bar- rel on firing between one rifle and another and so on. At least you are likely to avoid that infuriating moment when you find that the bullet you fired with such care missed the whole target and is wast- ed.

When you are satisfied by careful work on the range that your rifle is sighted-in exactly for what you need, then reinsert the collimator and make a note of the setting – so many squares up or sideways from the centre – and mark it on the collimator with a note of the ammunition used. Each load may well demand a different scope setting.

Once the setting is noted, the collimator can be used to check for any alteration in zero – if you have dropped the rifle, for example, or after any journey especially if you think that somebody has sat on it in the car or piled heavy luggage on top. Above all if you have had a shot which did not go where it ought to have done. Stick the collimator in the end of the barrel, check the reading and either be reassured that it was you (which it usually is) or find the zero is really out of kilter. In that case, stop stalking and find a place where you can have a few quiet shots and put the matter right. It's better to have a blank day than a wounded beast.

Stalking clothes

Jackets and trousers
The woodland stalker needs a lightweight jacket which is wind- and waterproof. Extra padding can be added underneath for cold weather. The finish must be soft; harsh or waxy materials make loud, deer-scaring noises when you push past twigs or spiky greenery like Sitka spruce. 'Breathable' garments stop one getting sweaty during a trying stalk and then chilled if the beast makes you wait about for a shot. Over the years jackets and other items of clothing in disruptive (camouflage) patterns have become accepted gear among woodland stalkers. Much of it came from army-surplus stores in the first place, followed by purpose-made

garments in roughly the same pattern and colours. Some of these were designed for jungle-fighting and were too bright. Remember that deer have little colour vision beyond a few yards but the general *tone* of your clothing must conform reasonably to the type of woodland you are in. Remember, too, that cloth tends to darken as it gets wet, so that a jacket which looks part of the landscape when you set out can stand out like a bluebottle on a blanket if it starts to teem with rain. We also have a public relations problem to consider: a patterned stalking coat may look very practical in our eyes, but to Joe Public someone armed and in 'cammo' clothing is a terrorist. Stalkers like to keep a low profile, which is not improved by panic calls to the police.

If the woods where you stalk are not infested with walkers, joggers, birdwatchers and old ladies with wild dogs, you are lucky and can happily wear 'cammo'. All that is advisable is to take off the compromising garment when you reach the car. Most stalkers are not so fortunate, and would be well advised to look at some of the less meaningful alternatives.

How about good old tweed? It is unobtrusive, makes you look like a harmless country chap, and plenty of jackets are available which keep the wet out completely. Make sure about washability – the mix of wool and plastics may offer difficulties, and stalking is a messy business. Jackets made of fleece have been around for some

time, but now one can combine the noiselessness of fleece with a sandwiched breathable waterproof layer. Nomad of Aberfeldy make a range of stalker-designed clothes which are well worth a look.

The Continental tradition is dark green loden cloth, which blends in well with a gloomy autumn spruce forest but looms black and obvious against spring greenery or the golden colours of our mixed woodland later on. The green woollen Swanndri coat is excellent and noiseless for stalking in thick conifer plantations as one does in the north, though it is too warm for summer work.

Taking a steady look through the binoculars using a stalking stick. A warm outfit for winter weather: Musto Goretex jacket, Aigle rubber boots and thermal gloves.

Trousers again must be soft. Even corduroy is hopelessly noisy in the stillness of the woods. If you fancy them, breeks or plus-fours are fine for autumn and winter work, but from spring to late summer woollen stockings will pick up an unwelcome crop of ticks with uncomfortable results. Besides their bloodsucking, they carry the agent of Lyme Disease which can be communicated to man.

Footwear

I have to confess that I have never found the ideal shoe or boot for the purpose! To a great extent it is a matter of horses for courses; hot and dry or cold and stony and wet, there isn't any real compromise. Of course, the important thing is to help you to keep quiet, not to blister or bruise the soles of your feet and still be comfortable after three or four hours' stalking.

Thick soles will not let you feel the presence of a twig before your weight has cracked it. Thin soles are agony on stony ground and may slip in the wet. Waterproof shoes or boots get uncomfortably hot, but on boggy ground or for walking through dew- or rain-soaked grass anything less is a misery; very soon they start to squelch at every pace you take. Walking through heather one must have some protection – either high boots or separate leggings fitting tight over the shoe uppers – otherwise the seed heads work down into the most uncomfortable corners and make sores. Ticks, too, need to be kept out as far as possible in the summer when they swarm on the grass, waiting for a lift and a feed.

What can one suggest? For dry summer evenings on easy going something like boat shoes or trainers are good, provided the soles are fairly thin. Colour is probably less

The woollen Swanndri jacket is noiseless, even when brushing through Sitka spruce.

important than for other items of clothing. For the same country the next morning one would be more comfortable in lightweight high-laced Goretex (or similar) boots, or even a lightweight pair of green wellies, provided they fit tightly round the calf. Old-fashioned gumboots make a galumphing noise as you walk because the legs are wide and stiff.

When the going is steep and tricky one has to have well-fitting boots with good ankle support and a gripping pattern on the sole. The latter must be rubber and not have studs or nails. Almost always you are likely to be working at close quarters with your quarry – and deer have exceptional hearing!

Gloves or mittens

Can you imagine getting your hands so cold that it is imperative to thrust them into the insides of a newly-shot deer, or the exquisite pain which follows from near-frostbite? Many Highland stalkers will sympathise, but even in the south-country woods things can get desperate, especially in wet snow. The trouble is that one has to be able to have bare-skin contact with the trigger but somehow retain enough feeling in the trigger finger for a controlled let-off.

I have tried most things in the way of gloves. When it is cold and dry one can use those elegant leather shooting gloves with a slit in the first finger but if it rains they are like frozen spinach wrapped round your hands. Woollen fingerless mitts are better, and quite a good compromise except for extreme conditions. I had them with very long cuffs, because if the blood gets chilled between jacket sleeve and glove, your hands will be cold whatever you have on them. A thin pair is also good to shield the betraying flash of bare hands in the summer as one uses the binoculars and to ward off at least some of the biting flies which can be such a distracting plague. Knitted thermal gloves thin enough to make it possible to feel the trigger are a practical idea. They are surprisingly warm.

In really cold conditions, I tried a pair of big skiing mitts with a Thinsulate lining. They were delightfully warm and waterproof. The idea was that when faced with a shot one gripped the right hand mitt in your teeth and pulled it off. Like so many bright ideas, there were unexpected snags, usually the thing stuck half off because my hands were wet.

Hats

A hat with a broad brim is needed to shield your pale face, keep the rain off and prevent midges from getting at your scalp. When these pests are really bad you can drape a soft fine-mesh veil over the brim and tuck it into your shirt. This veil is also additional camouflage when you are calling a buck.

Stalking equipment

Carefully chosen equipment makes all the difference to your pleasure in stalking. Half asleep in the early morning it is all to easy to leave some vital piece of equipment behind. Keep a card with a list of essentials for a quick check. Mine is inside the gun safe: it is not likely you will forget the rifle!

Binoculars

Although a would-be stalker naturally thinks first about what rifle he should get, binoculars are equally or more important. Not only your enjoyment, but your effectiveness and ultimately whether you shoot safely or dangerously depend on them. There is a well-proved safety rule that you never point a firearm at anything which is not clearly identified and this is all-important when you are stalking in thick cover, in bad light and with a powerful rifle in your hands. If you use your scope as a substitute for binoculars, you are doing just that.

Binoculars have an identifying code, e.g. 8×30. As with scopes, the first figure refers to magnification, eight times (8×) in this case; the second gives the size of the object lens (30 mm). Many first-time buyers of binoculars fall for high power, but there are snags: high magnification increases not only the image size but also any shake from your hands. This cancels any theoretical advantage. Secondly, the field of view and the depth of focus are both smaller, so you can't be certain of picking up what you want to see at once, a vital point in woodland stalking, and even when you have located it, more time may be lost fiddling with the focus to get the image sharp enough.

Careful and leisured spying, especially over large-scale blocks like this Border forest, is more rewarding than long unplanned walks. *(Photo L Guthrie)*

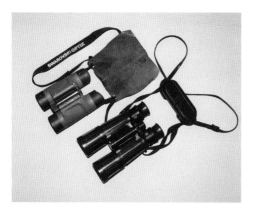

Two first-class binoculars for woodland stalking: Swarovski 7×30B (with leather flap for covering the eyepieces) and Zeiss 7×42.

A lot of stalking goes on at dusk and dawn, necessarily in bad light, so you want glasses that perform well at low light levels. In principle, the bigger the object lens the more light it lets through, though high-quality optical glass performs better than that used in mass-produced instruments. You usually get what you pay for, so get as good a pair as you can possibly afford. That said, the traditional type with a hump (*porro prism*) are simpler to make than the design with straight tubes (*roof prism*), so quality for quality, they are slightly cheaper.

As a guide, I have finally settled on 7×42 roof prism binoculars as a good compromise. Seven-power gives almost universal focus at normal stalking ranges and the 42 mm object lenses, admittedly in a first-class instrument, are large enough to give excellent dusk performance without making it cumbersome or heavy.

Knives for stalkers

Over the years I have bought a lot of knives and somehow I don't seem to have all of them now, though I can only remember once making the usual mistake of leaving it at the site of the gralloch. I suppose it is still under that birch tree in Wiltshire! After that loss (it was a favourite) I always tried to say 'Knife!' loudly to myself when about to set off with the beast on my back.

While a knife, or even two in case you lose one, makes an essential part of the stalker's equipment, do not think that you need to improve your macho image with a nine-inch Bowie hanging from your belt. In fact stalkers are well advised these days to keep a low profile and not leave themselves open to being mistaken for the local trouble-maker.

All we are looking for is a blade which is sharp, keeps its edge through a reasonable amount of work, is designed to do the job without risk to the operator and is small enough to be convenient. The choice is baffling: one is confronted by penknives, sheath knives, knives with lots of spare blades and other tools. What do we want a knife to do? First of all, keep it for deer work, not sharpening pencils, digging up turf and all the other ways of abusing an edge which ruin most knives. Every stalker is responsible

Stalking knife and folding saw. All items used for handling and dressing deer should be suitable for sterilising.

for ensuring that nothing is done which might contaminate the carcass, so a plastic-handled knife with a plastic sheath which can be sterilised is recommended. Bone-handled or folding knives are not. (Study Appendix 6 before making a choice.)

No beginner should attempt to finish off a wounded animal with his knife – a second shot is better, having due regard for safety in the heat of the moment. A dead beast should be bled by inserting a knife at the base of the neck to sever the blood vessels there even though a chest shot with modern rifle bullets usually gives massive internal bleeding.

Your stalking knife must be scalpel-sharp for performing the gralloch, its prime function. The sharper it is, the less you are liable to cut yourself, because less strength is needed. Later it has to help with skinning, a very knife-blunting operation. Neither job requires a very long blade. Something about 10 cm (4 in) is more than enough. It should be rounded towards the point.

If you try to cut either the pelvic bone or the breastbone with a knife made of very hard steel it may do it for a time but sooner or later you will chip the edge. Use a saw.

A sheath knife is uncomplicated and easily cleaned, but apart from the concealment issue mentioned already, one should be careful that it is secure in its sheath even in the event of a tumble, and cannot either fall out or push its point dangerously through the end. Any knife used for deer work, where one's hands will be slippery and possibly cold, should have a guard between handle and blade to avoid suddenly finding that you are gripping a very sharp blade rather than the handle. It can happen.

How does one keep that razor edge which most knives have when they are brand-new? Use a medium-to-fine oilstone and push the blade along it, as if you were trying to shave a thin slice off the stone. It sounds awful, but it works! The angle needs to be fairly flat, and after much use and sharpening a shoulder will develop which needs to be ground back before you attempt to resharpen. The other thing is not to use your good knife for things

Stalker's Reminder List

Rifle, bolt, sling, scope	Rubber gloves	Camera
Ammunition	Roe sack	Spare handkerchief
Binoculars	Midge veil	Money
Knife	Stalking jacket	Anti-midge
Hat	Roe calls	Poly bags
Gloves or mittens	Compass and map	Paper, pencil
Stick	String and rope	First aid
Small torch	Thermos	Toilet paper
Mobile phone – in case of accident	Folding saw	Firearm Certificate

It may seem a long list, but most of it packs neatly into pockets or the roe sack.

it was never designed for, such as cutting bone or wood. Use another one for the boy scout stuff.

Roe sacks and other means of transport

When a roe is shot it usually has to be carried some way, and it can be a heavy load unless you go prepared. If you do not mind

getting messy, the beast can be carried over your shoulder by trussing the legs together but it is a one-sided weight, the head of a buck prongs you in the leg and the rifle tends to slip off. Far better to have a large frameless rucksack known as a roe sack. It should be not less than 60×50 cm (24×20 in) and preferably bigger. It should have a removable washable liner, broad straps to distribute the weight and two

The roe sack (S Wright) on its washable lining. Note the strap and toggle, the chest-strap and the stout forged carrying ring at the top of the bag.

Even a heavy buck is an easy load when properly stowed in the roe sack.

pockets for various essential bits of equipment. One strap should unclip to help shouldering a heavy load.

Bipods
A bipod is a two-legged support for the fore-end of the rifle. There is nothing new about them – W. D. M. Bell, the famous elephant hunter, used his 'Karamojo stick', a short forked rest to shove into the ground for a steady prone shot. Stalking on open ground,

The Harris bipod (prone model). Longer models allow shots from a sitting position.

The late Edgar James, a great name in stalking, with a well-behaved spaniel. Without gloves note how the stalker's face and hands show up.

whether it happens to be fields or the open hill, almost always involves a prone shot, but very often with loose straw, growing crops, chunks of rock, heather or other hazards which need a certain amount of elevation if the bullet is to fly true. A crumbling tower of rifle case, binoculars and the lunch bag is no substitute for a bipod. Some stalkers have an uncomfortable feeling that bipods are somehow unsporting, but if you decide to shoot a beast, anything that helps to do this quickly and humanely cannot be unsporting.

For open-hill stalking the standard model with legs extending from 19 to 31 cm (7 to 12 in) is very practical, though on farmland one may feel the need for the long-legged model which allows an assisted sitting shot extending from 34 to 73 cm (13–29 in) to clear stubble turnips, combine straw or just humps in the ground.

There are some snags. One is that the rifle has to be levelled, which can involve some astonishing contortions to shorten one leg with the sliding adjustment without revealing oneself to the deer.

Full use should be made of informal shooting positions by constant practice. Cammo clothes help in concealment but can lead to misunderstandings with the public.

Some models overcome this by permitting a degree of tilt. Shooting accurately with a bipod needs practice. The jump is different, and one should lie prone more in line with the rifle than the standard 45-degree position. If the bipod is resting on very hard ground there may be a tendency to shoot high. The legs are spring-loaded, opening with an audible click, and shutting (if you are not careful) with the efficiency of a mousetrap. Experiment on the range to get these things ironed out before taking a shot at a deer.

A bipod needs to be attached to the forward sling swivel, the sling itself going on a corresponding eye below. One can have two swivels so that the bipod can be attached and removed without fiddling with the sling. They weigh between 295 and 485 g (10–17 oz), so leaving it on all the time adds noticeably to the rifle's slung weight and balance. However, fitting it on in the heat of the moment can be agonisingly slow. Compromise by having it on all the time for stalking in open fields or on the hill, but in the rucksack for fairly unlikely eventualities in the woods. If you are sitting down in ambush, that is another matter.

Stalking sticks

In thick woodland most shots will be taken off-hand at fairly short range. The deer will often be alerted and movement must be kept to a minimum. There is never a convenient tree to provide a rest! For these conditions a stick is very valuable. It should reach to

ABOVE LEFT: To use the stick effectively the rifle should be carried muzzle down.
MIDDLE: In this way the rifle can be raised with a minimum of movement.
ABOVE RIGHT: To make a steady shot off the stick, the feet should be somewhat apart to form a firm triangle with the base of the stick.

your forehead, thick enough not to bend when you lean on it and without any fork at the top. Use it to steady the binoculars for a good look and then to provide vertical support for the rifle so that all you have to control is the side-to-side swing.

The stick should be held in the left hand (for a right-hander) and so the rifle must be slung from the opposite shoulder, otherwise you just can't get it up without dropping your stick. Carry the rifle muzzle down and you can raise it with the minimum movement. Practise it. Mud or snow can be kept out by sticking a piece of plastic tape over the muzzle – it will not affect the ballistics or produce dangerous pressure as it would with a shotgun.

Unless you can jam it in the ground, the stick only gives stability in one plane. There is a tendency to sway from side to side which is why the double or split stick is popular. Some are marvels of ingenuity, but one can do very well with a couple of ⅜ in dowel rods or plastic garden canes hinged together with the rubber band off the family Hoover. If you don't have some means of keeping the other ends clipped together they will clatter, but whatever you use needs to be pushable-off with one foot!

Smoking
If a deer smells your smoke, he will have smelt you! So it doesn't matter from that point of view. A puff of smoke is the most delicate wind direction indicator besides keeping buzzing insects at bay. Non-smokers can use herbal cigarettes which smell (and taste) pretty strange but work just as well. In dry weather where there is a fire risk, do not indulge. In particular do not throw cigarette ends out of your high seat!

Spade
A camping-pattern folding spade should be kept in the car to help with burying the gralloch. When the car is stuck in snow, ice or mud you will be glad of it too.

Hearing protection
Every shot you take, or is discharged near you, damages your hearing. The effect is cumulative and irreversible, although actual deafness may not be apparent for a long time. The first essential is never to do range work or zeroing with unprotected ears. The form of protection depends to some extent on cost. Foam ear-plugs are the cheapest and possibly the least effective. Many shooters also find them uncomfortable. Non-active muffs work well but limit your hearing ordinary sounds. With electronic muffs one can hear everything, but loud noises are cut off below the level of damage, so that a shot is heard as a dull thud. To spend an entire stalking

outing in ear muffs, often with little prospect of a shot, might make one feel a bit ridiculous. To avoid this the only answer is to use hearing protectors which are made to fit into your ear like a hearing aid. They are very expensive, but how highly do you value a lifetime ability to hear?

Small but important items

Ammunition
Best kept in a compartmented leather pouch or an old soft purse to avoid rattling. Preferably one in the jacket pocket and a reserve in the roe sack. Take plenty: dealing with a wounded beast may use up several rounds or an emergency zeroing session may be needed. Make sure they are the right ones for the rifle!

Spare knife
In the roe sack, in case the main one gets lost or is blunt.

String and rope
A short length of each is always handy, the latter particularly if you plan to hang your beast in a tree for gralloching.

Handkerchief
Finding you have no handkerchief is a misery. Keep a spare in a poly bag.

First aid
A few Band-Aids in another poly bag. Serious gashes are not uncommon when dressing deer. For larger wounds the handkerchief and the poly bag itself can be used as a pad, secured in place with plaster. All stalkers should keep their tetanus jabs up to date.

Anti-midge
Poly bags
Liver, kidneys and heart are better removed from the carcass immediately, bagged and kept out of the flies.

Notebook and pencil
Essential not only for making occasional notes of what you have seen, but for the names and addresses of any suspicious characters you may meet, or the number of a loitering car. If you can't find a pencil at the critical moment, the soft lead tip of a bullet serves the purpose.

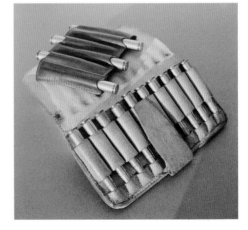

Two practical non-rattle pouches for ammunition.

Rubber gloves

The onus on all stalkers is to minimise the risk of contaminating the carcass, so all stalkers should use rubber gloves when gralloching. Latex examination gloves can be bought in bulk at most chemists.

High seats

High seats have three main advantages. From an elevated perch much more can be seen than from ground level, shooting is safer in

A metal four-leg high seat, in this case steadied additionally by roping to the tree.

flat or populated country because the shot is downwards, and if they are properly designed with a good support for the rifle the actual shot is easier. They also encourage the stalker to stay put and let the deer come to him.

For short-term use a portable seat is extremely useful. There are two basic designs, either two-legged to prop against a tree, or self-standing with four legs. Portable seats are made of aluminium or steel. Aluminium models are very light, rather delicate and relatively expensive. Steel seats are cheaper but heavier, and need annual painting and maintenance to keep them safe. Alternatively seats can be made of wood, which is heavier still but less desirable in the eyes of a thief. To comply with safety regulations, among other things timber seats need to be constructed with the ladder rungs notched into the uprights and wired up and down the uprights and along each rung. Seats made of green timber soon rot and become dangerous; peeled, seasoned wood is essential. Pressure-creosoted or Celcured timber is the best of all and will last for years.

Modern safety requirements dictate that great care has to be taken in the design, construction, use and maintenance of all high seats. Those made of timber may require even greater care and a written schedule for regular inspection and maintenance is insisted on by the authorities regardless of who might use them, prime responsibility lying with the occupier of the land. Look carefully at Appendix 6.

Lean-to seats to accommodate two people are difficult to design but this is necessary where paying guests are to be taken out by the stalker. Any seat must be safe and comfortable, with a broad seat, a rest for the feet and a rail or table on which to steady the

Wooden lean-to two-man seat. To comply with present-day safety regulations the rungs must be notched into the uprights and wired both ways. Maintenance has to follow a written schedule.

Where rising ground gives a good view a 'low seat' is useful. *(Photo I Allman)*

rifle for a shot. The rungs of the ladder should not be too far apart, so that it can be mounted easily and unobtrusively by elderly guests, or by the stalker himself when a buck is already aware of him. Box high seats should be made with a slit through which one can observe and shoot, otherwise the general effect resembles a Punch and Judy show which even the most unsophisticated roe is liable to notice.

A useful tower seat can be made with Bantam scaffolding sections fitted at the top with a wooden floor and seat and shielded with wood or camouflage netting. Guy wires are essential, as they are for any seat in an exposed or windy place. Generally, a height to the seat of between 3 and 4 m (9–12 ft) is ample.

Seats in trees are rarely satisfactory or comfortable, and few indeed comply with modern safety rules. Usually the only suitable tree is not in the best position for a seat and making it involves using nails, which certainly is not popular with the forester, or anyone using a chainsaw.

Placing and use

The main thing about placing high seats is not to put a permanent one up until you are sure that you need it. Many seats are erected

A high seat constructed from scaffolding.

in a fit of enthusiasm and never get used. Others quickly become useless because of the rapid growth of the crop they were designed to protect, or summer weeds such as bracken effectively hide the deer for half the year.

A permanent seat represents quite an investment and should only be sited where a number of deer are likely to be shot from it every year. This usefulness must last for most of the life of the seat, that is for ten years or so. Potential sites should be tried out with portable or semi-portable seats until the need for something permanent becomes obvious. Portable seats can also be used to cope with temporary problems such as the control of deer going out on to a particular farm crop, or for taking individual bucks. Once the buck has been shot, the seat can be moved and used in another location.

One should be able to approach and get into a seat without disturbing deer which are lying up or feeding nearby. It may be possible to place them on ride intersections so that they can be approached with due regard to the wind, or approach paths can be cut from the nearest access track. If at all possible the seat should not be silhouetted against the sky but have a background of taller trees, otherwise the slightest movement in the seat will be observed. When making seats a tall stalker should remember that some of his guests may be short and some slightly more rotund.

Sitting for two hours on a plank that is just too high can be agonising and a shooting slit at the wrong height will merely lead to missed or wounded animals. The entry port to a box high seat should not be so narrow that it is a squeeze. Lean-to high seats need a very substantial tree because otherwise the slightest wind will set them swaying and make accurate shooting very difficult. One can cure the trouble by cutting off the top above the seat – but only after due consultation!

It is worth going to quite a lot of trouble to make every hour spent in a high seat worthwhile. One way is to put the seat up where the deer are likely to be and where they can be seen. Alternatively make the place as attractive to deer as you can and

The ultimate luxury! A transportable high seat which could have real utility especially for farm crop protection.

bring them to you. A small amount of scrub clearance can make a useful clearing, and hopefully with suitable species the cut stumps will regenerate into attractive coppice growth. A thin strip running away from the seat is better than the same cleared area round its feet. If the clearing crosses various deer paths so much the better. Salt licks on the whole are unsuccessful, but planting or encouraging a few bushes of willow or rowan, especially in conifer areas, will attract the deer and hold them where they can be seen.

Remember the direction of the prevailing wind when deciding where to put a seat and try to arrange things so that you are not staring into the rising or setting sun.

In addition to the regular checks under the Health and Safety regulations (see Appendix 6) before the beginning of the buck season and again in October, each seat should be visited for routine housekeeping. Branches may have drooped down, interfering with the arcs of fire. Farther out, pruning may be necessary if the best places can no longer be seen. The access track may need to be cut back again and any loose twigs brushed away. Anything which is likely to make your time in the seat safer, more comfortable and more productive should be anticipated. If you or your visitors smoke, a jar should be kept for cigarette ends to avoid the risk of starting a fire.

PART 6

Stalking Technique

Still-hunting

The accepted way of stalking a roe in thick woodland is to drift very slowly and silently along the paths and rides up or across the wind, planning where to put each foot to avoid noise and at the same time spying all round for the slight indications which are all

Thick cover like this could conceal any number of deer. Slow progress is everything.

that an experienced stalker needs to spot the presence of a deer. Obviously the technique is most easily learned by persuading an expert stalker to take you out. If that is not possible, try to join one of the practical training courses organised by B.D.S. and B.A.S.C. There is all the difference in the world between theory and practice! One needs both. You will also be shown how to take care over your shooting even in the fever heat of excitement, and to gralloch a beast neatly to produce venison which is clean and wholesome.

Once out on your own it just doesn't seem so simple. Even skilled stalkers take time to get to know a bit of ground so that they can predict to some extent where a deer may show up. Go much more slowly than you ever thought, plan your movement up- or across the wind, and take each corner s-l-o-w-l-y, stopping to rake each new view with the binoculars. Remember that once on the ground, you are just as likely to see a deer where you are as anywhere else – so why hurry past it? A glance behind often discloses a deer which has watched you go past before getting up. Start to feel undressed without the binoculars round your neck, they are your passport to success in seeing deer, and to ensuring that every shot you take is safe. There is also a great deal of pleasure to be had from watching other wildlife about their affairs in the woods.

The best chance of a buck is in the magical hours around dawn

A dog with a good nose, like this German shorthaired pointer, will point deer that would otherwise be passed by – but only those upwind of you!

in the summer and again in the evening until the light fades. As local knowledge builds up you will visit or scan places where deer can be expected to appear; maybe in the fields in the spring, on the edge of the moor or on sunny banks and streamsides.

No matter how carefully you work upwind, the wash of scent you send down the wind behind you will eventually tell all the deer in the wood that you have been about. Deer are not fools. They learn quickly and will soon fail to appear at the expected times and places. So vary your technique, your route and your hours and do not visit the same area too often. Constant disturbance by over-keen stalking will make the deer chary of appearing at all during the hours when they expect you. They will become increasingly shy and elusive, feeding at night and during full daylight – when you have gone!

Most chances of a shot in thick woodland will be at comparatively close range: there the deer is! It is probably at least half alerted and you will probably have to take the shot from where you are, with the minimum of movement, or risk losing the chance. Standing, kneeling or sitting shots are the rule. The best that you can hope for is to reach a tree from which a steady shot can be taken. Incidentally, never rest the rifle against anything solid, such as a tree or stone, without your hand or a coat between as a cushion or the shot will go wide. Prone shots, normal in hill-stalking are the exception in woodland. Standing or off-hand shots require practice and should not be taken beyond 50 metres. They can be made much more steady with the help of a stick as described on page 94.

Still-hunting demands absolute concentration, so that the slightest noise, the smallest movement in the bushes or the least spot of an odd colour will be investigated and checked, if necessary with the binoculars. Lots of deer get shot by chance but the consistently successful stalker must forecast in his mind what the deer will be doing according to the time of year, the weather and the state of the moon, and then go and see if he is right or not. Then he has to have the woodcraft to arrive on the scene unobserved, plus the skill and self-discipline to wait for a certain shot and make it good.

In winter the deer will behave differently and may be found in different places. Days are short and stalking hours coincide with the working day, so even greater care has to be taken to make sure no one is about. Farm crops are a draw when food in the woods runs low. At sunrise after a cold night deer may often be found on sunny banks where they like to move about and get warm. Crusted snow makes stalking a nightmare, and it may be necessary to face some very cold vigils in temporary high seats when everything crunches like the icing on a wedding cake.

Sitting

Good relations with the people who are about the woods and fields (often cemented with an occasional gift of a liver or bit of venison) will soon bring in reports of where deer are regularly seen: the family party every evening in that field, always a buck in such-and-such a clearing, fraying damage just starting in the young pines. These reports are enormously helpful, particularly if you are not on the ground all the time, and even though descriptions of individual deer may be pretty inaccurate. Sitting down quietly to watch what happens then becomes worthwhile. A knowledge of the habits and movements of deer can be built up much more quickly by quietly watching than by moving about, disturbing their normal routine as you go.

A high seat may be necessary to overlook the spot, or to shoot safely. One of the pleasures of sitting in a high seat is that woodland creatures soon forget you are there and can be seen about their normal affairs. Most stalkers use high seats more in the evenings, getting into place well before dusk, but providing the access has been well organised one can be in a high seat before first light without disturbing feeding deer and get the full advantage of that first hour when their vigilance may, if ever, be slightly relaxed.

Some comfort is essential if one is to sit nearly motionless for a long time, otherwise you start to twitch or to get bored just when the deer might be expected to move. Flies and midges can be a torment. One needs to be covered up as far as possible, particularly

A quiet sitting shot across the field.

Prone shots are uncommon in the woods.

ankles, hands, neck and head, with the additional help of a good repellent such as Jungle Formula. In winter keeping warm and dry can be a problem. Surgeons' thin rubber gloves under a pair of woollen ones make a surprisingly warm combination, especially when backed up by a pair of the small chemical hand-warmers which never fail to work. Put additional clothing in the roe sack so that you do not get overheated walking out to your seat, and remember to put it on before you start to feel chilled.

Moving

There are occasions when stalking can be supplemented by carefully organised moves to get extra does during the short winter days. Properly carried out, the deer are encouraged to move gently along their accustomed paths where they may be ambushed by waiting riflemen. It is best done in January and February when the older bucks will already have enough velvet to make them readily distinguishable.

A succession of small copses such as are often found on pheasant shoots can be effectively combed out. Deer will hesitate inside cover before making up their minds to break for the next wood, and having started at a run will hesitate outside the next wood, and again inside it. So there are three potential places where from ground level or a high seat shots at stationary or slow-moving deer can be expected.

The range is likely to be short and a very low-power scope sight, or a variable which can be set to between 1× and 3× at its lowest setting, gives the necessary wide field and clear aiming mark. Nevertheless, self-control in only taking the most certain

Look before you shoot! The roe tail-on has no anal tush, showing that it is actually a buck, and the other shows the bumps of growing pedicles. *(Photo J Poutsma)*

shots is essential and only experienced rifles should take part. One unarmed walker to get the deer on the move is all that is required, possibly with a close-ranging dog if the cover is very thick. One or more rifles, depending on the size of the woodland, take up previously planned positions and must not move away until the manoeuvre is over. Although the rifles must only be stationed where they can shoot with safety, the walker should be provided with a horn or whistle to indicate his whereabouts and he should wear an orange or light-coloured coat. There should be no noise or shouting, if anything just an occasional tap of a stick.

Moving can sometimes be employed in the summer to outwit a buck or to shift him from a place where a shot cannot be taken, such as a garden, and also in the unfortunate event of a wounded animal taking refuge in thick cover.

Each move should only be attempted once or at most twice a year. Deer are quick to learn. Something that works well the first time and results in a shot will probably be blank if it is tried again too soon afterwards.

Calling

Roe deer life is dominated by the female, even during the rut. If a doe finds herself without a consort she will go and find one, bringing him back to where she wants to rut. If he tries to wander off she will do her best to stop him.

To see a buck chasing a doe round and round makes one think that he is in control. Not so: she is egging him on with small squeaks of encouragement. If the buck stops running you can be quite sure that the doe will not take the opportunity of making her escape! To attract a buck various female noises can be imitated, some of which may not be heard in a lifetime of stalking. Calling is much more likely to work if there is a doe in season somewhere in the vicinity. Bucks may come to the call as early as the first week in July, and odd hopefuls will turn up from time to time well into September. But the real time when calling is worthwhile is likely to lie between 20 July and 15 August, depending on the year and the weather at the time. Too many calling experiments before things are really stirring merely educate the deer, which realise that something fishy is going on.

Calling works best from about 8.00 a.m. to 3.00 p.m. and is more likely to produce results in hot or thundery weather. Providing it is warm, rain does not seem to matter but windy or cold weather is usually hopeless. In choosing a place to call do not expect too much of a buck. Unless he is quite fevered with the rut he will prefer to come quietly, weighing up the situation before committing himself to the open. A place which is open enough to allow the buck to be seen at a reasonable range but with bushes or undergrowth to make him feel safe is worth trying, particularly if you know that there is a territorial buck in the area. Slight noises may actually attract his attention but once the caller is standing against a tree, or sitting if that gives the best visibility, he should keep very still indeed. The buck's sense of location is very accurate and all his senses will be on the alert, though one has to say that a buck in full rut sometimes seems to lose his sense of smell and comes boldly upwind. A veil over the face and gloves to shield the hands are advisable.

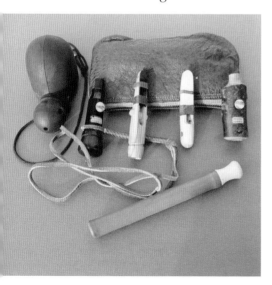

An unaccompanied doe attracts bucks to her by squeaking, which she continues during the ensuing chases. Even louder cries may be made when the tables are reversed and the buck starts to press his attentions on her. These phases of the rut can be imitated using a beech leaf if you have been taught that

Six well-tried calls. Left to right: Buttolo; Hubertus plastic; Austrian two-ended reed call; RP reed call; Hubertus cherry-wood. Below: Hungarian tube call. The spring lanyard can fit any call to prevent loss.

A stretched beech leaf is the traditional way to call roe.

difficult art, or otherwise with various whistles which can be bought or made.

While courting is in progress, the kid is safely bedded in the undergrowth where it will stay unless disturbed. Frightened, for example by a fox, the kid makes a high squeaking roughly in time with his breathing, which should bring the doe up to see what the trouble is. If she is with a buck he will come too. A doe coming into season makes a similar squeak but lower in pitch which is often repeated for many minutes while she walks through the wood in search of a mate. Rather more agonised squeals may be needed to detach a buck who is already in company with a doe. This last sound can only be counterfeited by a call which incorporates a stop so that a two-tone squeak can be made, or with the type that has an open reed which requires practice to master but is in the end the most effective and versatile. Because these noises are heard so rarely by the average stalker, learning calling is difficult without having the technique demonstrated. Making the best of a variety of calls is always a focus of interest at training courses. An audio cassette on calling roe is available.

Deciding what to shoot

A simple shooting plan was laid out in the section on management (page 49), which cuts through a lot of the mystique of selective shooting and is based on the known facts of roe biology.

Yearlings are not too difficult to tell from their seniors by their light bodies, legs long in proportion, thin necks and weak hind-quarters. The expression is innocent and Bambi-ish. Middle-age

Age classes in the buck cull	
Yearlings	60%
Middle-aged bucks	20%
Old bucks	20%

More than half a managed buck cull should consist of yearlings. *(Photo Sylvan Films)*

sees the body thicken; the jaw strengthens and the line of the back tends to become straighter (see illustration page 56). A buck in old age has a heavy forepart, a thick, short neck and strong hindquarters with a back line practically straight when unalarmed from ears to target, so that he resembles a good beef bullock in miniature.

Unfortunately, roe vary in body development as much as we do. One can get fat young bucks and thin old ones, so mistakes in selection will always be made. For this reason an allowance of 50 per cent error is made in the shooting plan. If no more than two middle-aged bucks are shot by mistake for each two old bucks, then you are doing quite well. Yearlings should be recognisable as such most of the time.

Allowance should also be made for the fact that the necks of the bucks thicken before the rut, giving them an appearance of age during July and August which they may not merit. Each buck that is shot should be carefully examined for evidence of age so that fewer mistakes are made as your experience builds up. (See *Healthy and unhealthy deer,* page 121).

The mistaken but widely held idea that roe can be selected for shooting by their antlers is so deeply ingrained that it is necessary to repeat the basic truth that ***antler growth is so variable from year to year to be quite useless for management purposes***. Age class, body size and condition are the only reliable indicators for a logical decision on whether or not to shoot. The objects of management as laid out on page 49 can only be achieved by shooting the right number and the right proportion in each age class. If large numbers of yearling bucks appear in summer from big

Middle-aged bucks should mostly be spared. Note the firm body line and strong neck. *(Photo Sylvan Films)*

woods nearby you will have to increase the number of them in the cull without shooting more mature animals, which are likely to be residents.

The doe cull

Culling does is the only effective way of regulating the population. To keep the population stable slightly more does than bucks should be shot each year. To reduce deer density, increase the doe cull. Any attempt at selecting the right doe to take out is pointless unless very few need to be shot. (See *What does to cull?*, page 56.) It is far more important to cull the correct number, otherwise your attempts at enlightened management will only result in an increase in the population followed by heavier mortality in the spring. Better a humane bullet than death by starvation or disease.

In most places November and the first half of December are difficult times to get many deer, particularly on pheasant shoots where there is much disturbance at that time of year. The game-keeper, too, may want the woods kept quiet. If a start has to be left until the New Year all kids can be assumed to be fully indepen-dent, though time will be short to complete the cull.

To make up for the additional difficulties of weather and short days the season in Scotland extends into March, when the deer are usually active and completion of the doe cull is fairly straight-

Saggy back, rounded hindquarters and sloping coronets show this to be an old buck. *(Photo Sylvan Films)*

forward. Many people are reluctant to shoot deer that are within three months of fawning. However, the stalker's first duty is to the living kid of the previous year rather than the unborn foetus. Only those who have been hampered for one reason or another in getting their quota need shoot does in March if they are concerned on this point. In England and Wales the season closes at the end of February.

Once having decided that an animal is shootable, the stalker must still consider these paramount points:

- Is it a safe shot?
- Are you near enough and steady enough to make a sure shot?
- Would it give a better chance if you wait a bit?

When in doubt do not shoot.

The shot and after

Shooting positions
If you go out with an experienced stalker, when he has the chance of a shot you will see that he gets as near as the beast will allow him and then gets into as comfortable and steady a position as

possible. He will not take a standing shot if he can take it prone or sitting. In thick woodland where standing shots have to be taken he will use a stick or move to a tree if one is near enough. Gate and fence posts are also very valuable, but you need to know how to use all these aids to their best advantage. It all needs practice, and this can be done without actually shooting, in the garden, on your stalking ground after the morning's stalk is over or on the range as part of a zero or practice session. All the contortions needed to get into position need to be totally familiar before trying it with a suspicious animal in full sight. Regardless of the actual range, *if you are not steady on the target area – do not fire.*

Where to aim

The vital areas of a roe are shown on the diagram on page 25. No one should try to take fancy shots at a deer, and the beginner should confine himself to getting his bullet into the ribcage in front of the diaphragm, which is difficult enough. The neck is small and mobile and only hits in the spine or the blood vessels are fatal. Head shots from the side should *never* be attempted. Usually the only effect is to break the jaw, producing an agonising wound which in the end leads to death by starvation. Hit in the lower part of the heart a beast will usually run from 15 to 50 m before collapsing. This is acceptable on the open hill or downland but in thick cover of any sort may mean a long search or even a lost animal. Keep your bullet up and forwards a trifle and your buck will drop on the spot. It is better to spoil the meat on the far shoulder and find your buck than to waste the whole carcass because it cannot be found immediately and is spoiled.

Reload immediately you have fired so that the noise of working the rifle bolt merges with the sound of the bullet, but do not dash in after a shot. If the beast struggles up you will be better placed for a steady second shot where you are, and if it is badly wounded but not dead, the sight of a human approaching may frighten it enough to get up and run off. So be deliberate; approach the place carefully with rifle loaded and ready. Even an apparently

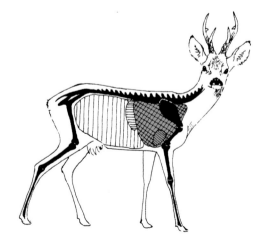

The vital area.

Avoid all chancy and trick shots. Wait for a broadside chance and aim as indicated.

dead animal may revive after being stunned by the shot touching the spine. Check that the beast is dead by touching the eye, preferably with your stick. If there is no reaction you can proceed with the gralloch.

Pay the greatest attention to the behaviour of the animal. The place where it was standing should be identified and if there is any doubt of the result a marker should be left where the shot was taken from as a reference point. In the case of flight listen intently to get the line, hoping all the time to hear the welcome sound of a crash in the bushes which will indicate that the beast has collapsed. If shot in the liver, stomach or intestines the animal will hump characteristically and go off slowly. It will probably lie up quickly unless disturbed, and the greatest care is needed in deciding what to do and how long to wait before taking any action.

If a search has to be made later with a dog, pieces of paper or plastic tape should be left to mark where you and the beast were standing. Try not to foil the scent by trampling about everywhere. Often a wounded animal will travel in a circle before collapsing or lying up, or make downhill to water.

Paint and pins

These are the two old terms for traces of blood and hair which can be found at the site of the shot and which may give one a good insight into the location of the wound, the likely behaviour of the animal and what should be done to retrieve the situation if it is not dead on the spot. The area should be searched very thoroughly because even after a fatal hit a small-calibre rifle may produce little evidence on the spot. Many animals are wasted every year because the shooter has not bothered to go and search, convinced he has missed. The buck may be lying dead within a few paces.

On snow-covered ground the smallest trace can of course be seen, and this is the best schoolroom for learning what to look for under more difficult circumstances. Arterial blood is scarlet and a good splash probably indicates a heart shot and a fatal run. Lung blood is pinkish and frothy, indicating a mortal shot and usually a short search. Traces of rumen contents or greenish blood indicates a hit in the liver or stomach, while a broken limb often bleeds extensively on the spot, maybe with fragments of bone, but bleeding soon declines to a few spots. Retrieving the wounded animal, unless you are very lucky, will mean getting a dog or, if it is known to have lain up in a patch of cover, organising a move.

To wait or not
The only time when quick action is necessary is in the unfortunate event of an animal seen to go away with a leg swinging; then every effort should be made to shoot it before it is out of sight. In all other circumstances one can afford to be deliberate. If the animal goes straight down but then starts to struggle, it could have been stunned and a quick second shot will be necessary. If you are confident of a heart or lung shot but the animal cannot be seen then a wait of five minutes or so will allow it to expire quietly. Hits far back in the body will probably make the animal lie up fairly quickly. A wait of up to a couple of hours may allow the animal to die without moving again. The difficulty is with shots taken late in the evening. A decision to wait may mean returning in the morning only to find after a warm summer night that putrefaction has already started and the meat is spoiled. Modern scope sights allow shots to be taken in very poor light indeed but the muzzle flash blinds the shooter and he finds immediately afterwards that all is dark and finding a dead buck is extremely difficult. The nightly close time starts one hour after sunset and should be observed for this reason, if for no other, even though before the shot you convince yourself that you can see clearly through the scope.

Dispatching wounded deer

A wounded animal that shows signs of getting away should have a second shot immediately, regardless of any possible damage to the carcass. One that shows signs of life when approached cautiously should be dispatched with a bullet at 10 m (30 ft) or so. Remember that the bullet will be 2 or 3 cm (¾–1 in) low at this range because of the height of the scope over the barrel, and remember too that the shot must be a safe one. Attempting to finish off a deer with a knife may galvanise it into action and needs skill which is better demonstrated by an expert. If the deer appears to be dead, approach it from behind and put one foot firmly on the neck or an antler, at the same time grasping the uppermost foreleg with one hand. Even if the animal then struggles, it can do you no harm. If it does not, touch the eye. If there is no reaction it is dead. Unload the rifle and put it down safely where it will not get knocked over, trodden on or unnecessarily wet.

A clean gralloch

To see anyone haggling and hauling at a dead deer as if he were disembowelling it by main strength is a horrible sight. With a sharp knife and a little science the thing can be done as a job of neat surgery with a minimum of gore. It has to be done promptly and thoroughly so that the meat is not contaminated and has the best chance of cooling quickly. You should return from your successful stalking expedition with a carcass which has been thoroughly cleaned out and well on the way to being in every way fit for human consumption. Think first about your shot placement: it is not nearly well enough recognised that the best venison comes from an unsuspecting beast which has been killed instantly by a bullet which produces massive internal bleeding. If it was alarmed, inflamed by the rut or not killed cleanly, the quality of the venison will suffer. Next, the job must be done quickly. I know that one can make a neater job in the larder, but in hot weather at least the process of deterioration starts at once and after half an hour the beast will be blown and probably cats' meat quality. No time should be wasted once a deer is dead in getting on with the gralloch.

Every effort should be made to keep a carcass clean. Hanging it up to drain and dry off is good practice – provided it still there when you come back!

What to Keep in the Roe Sack

- Spare knife
- Thin, strong rope
- Rubber gloves
- Compass
- Torch
- Midge repellent
- Poly bags
- A few spare rounds in pouch
- Handkerchief (in plastic bag)
- Band-Aid (in plastic bag)
- Toilet paper (in plastic bag)

The two pockets in your roe sack should contain some vital items for the gralloch and also a few spares for emergencies, as indicated in the box.

Every stalker has his own way of making a clean gralloch. The method depends on whether there is a convenient tree or bush from which you can suspend the carcass or if it has to be done on the ground. Suspending is regarded as 'best practice' but may be impossible where there are no suitable trees. The preliminaries are the same for both.

Make sure the animal is dead by touching an eyeball. Put on the rubber gloves. Bleed the animal with a thrust of the knife at the base of the neck. Turn it on its back, pinch up the belly skin and make a careful incision without puncturing the rumen beneath. After this always cut from the inside towards the fur. Cut forwards to the breastbone (sternum) and down to the groin, removing the udder if it is a doe, or lifting and freeing the genitals back to the anus if it is a male. Make a circular cut round the anus and cautiously separate the end of the gut and the genitalia where they pass through the pelvis. Empty any pellets from the end of the gut. Some stalkers try to open up the aitchbone with a knife point. This almost always results in puncturing the bladder.

With the beast lying on its back, pull the rumen and gut half out, and push the genitals and rectum forward into the body cavity. Slit up the neck and separate the gullet and windpipe right up to the tongue. Tie the gullet in a knot to avoid material from the rumen being forced out like toothpaste from a tube and pull it through, leaving the heart and lungs in front of the diaphragm. Lift out the whole digestive tract; remove the liver and kidneys. This can be done very well if there is a convenient tree from which the beast can be hung with the rope in your roe sack.

Approach the beast from behind. Touch an eyeball: if there's no reaction it is dead. Do not attempt to finish a beast off with a knife – take a safe shot from short range. Hygiene regulations insist on bleeding, which is done as shown, holding the leg and inserting the knife at the base of the neck. *(Photo M Swan)*

Put the liver and kidneys in separate poly bags, ready for trimming and washing before being rebagged and labelled for the freezer when you get home – unless of course you feel like a real hunter's breakfast when you get back. Roe liver sliced and fried, with an egg and fried bread is food for the gods, or for those of them that hunt, anyway!

Allow the beast to drain for a few minutes then introduce it, backside-first and legs-up, into the roe sack. It may be easier to put it in the liner to begin with, then lift this package into the main rucksack. As soon as you get to the car, decant the carcass into a big, clean open-topped plastic box so that it can cool. Remember to bury the gralloch (badger setts are handy, and the inhabitants won't turn up their noses at the offering). Walkers do not appreciate the sight, and their dogs may do a bit of very inconvenient retrieving if the remains have just been hidden.

The minute you get back the carcass has to be hung up to dry and set in a ventilated place, free from the attentions of cats, dogs, rats and above all bluebottles. Open up the chest cavity by cutting round the diaphragm and remove the lungs and heart. Note the path of your bullet and the damage, relating this to the animal's behaviour after the shot for future reference. You must also look carefully for evidence of disease or parasites, especially in the lungs, lymph nodes and liver (see *Healthy and unhealthy deer – what to look for* on page 121, and Appendix 6).

Given safe storage, the carcass can be left to hang unskinned for two or three days, longer in really cold weather. In the dog days of

A neat gralloch on the ground demonstrated on a fallow buck by professional stalker Mike Small. Make the first cut, guarding the knife point with two fingers to avoid puncturing the rumen.

Cut round the anus without puncturing the genitals or gut. Empty the last part of the gut. Free off and push the genital tract and rectum carefully back into the body cavity. If there is a suitable tree, later stages can be done after the beast has been hung up by the hocks.

Slit up the throat, separate the windpipe and gullet and remove them complete with the tongue.

Tie up the gullet to prevent rumen contents from leaking.

Pull the gullet through the chest cavity, leaving the heart and lungs in place.

Lift the complete digestive tract away, ready for loading the carcass in the roe sack.

summer something really has to be done at least by next morning or it will go rotten. All offal needs to be dealt with quickly before it deteriorates. Kidneys are better frozen in their covering of fat, if any. For immediate use they need to be halved lengthways so that the protective skin can be peeled off and with it the duct and white pipe-work leading to the centre. Some people find the taste of kidneys rather strong; in that case soak them in a little milk overnight. I think they are so good painted with olive oil, sprinkled with paprika and gently grilled that it seems a pity just to add them to a stew. Hearts make the finest mince and should be dealt with before going into the freezer to save space. Cut the valve-work off the top and slice the big muscle into strips preparatory to mincing. A Magi-mix does the job in seconds. A whole liver may be too much to unfreeze at a time, but it can be sliced first and bagged in suitable portions.

Healthy and unhealthy deer – what to look for

Looking first at the antlers of a dead buck is quite natural. We need to check our assessment of them before the shot and maybe to see how the newest trophy compares with others in the collection. Trophy hunting is not dishonourable providing that it is secondary to carrying out a plan of management. The idiosyncrasies of antler growth make a buck's headgear the most individual part of him. Old friends can be recognised at least during the current year, though you often realise that you have never seen the buck before.

Previous estimates of age can now be checked, first by the external appearances. Facial coloration in younger bucks tends to be clear-cut, while an old buck often has a grizzled face. He will also have a patch of rather curly hair just in front of his antlers, rather like a bull. In younger bucks this is smooth.

Expose the teeth by slitting up one side of the cheek. Each side of the jaw has four incisors (there are none in the upper jaw), the last of these is a modified canine tooth. There is then a gap, three premolars and three molars, all adapted for chewing the cud. If the front premolar has three parts or cusps this is a milk tooth and indicates that the animal is less than one year old. This milk tooth is usually shed about May but the date varies. By the same date the last true molar will have erupted at the back of the jaw. The molars in a young animal are high and sharp, wearing down with age and use until they are flattened, showing large areas of brown dentine and nearly level with the gum. Tooth wear is very irregular, depending on the type of food and the grittiness of the soil.

Wear on the incisors usually indicates an animal which has been feeding mainly on heather. The molars can become worn and flattened at any age between five and twelve. *Diagrams relating wear to age are very misleading.* Other more definite indications of age can be seen when the head is boiled out and one can also tell to some extent by the toughness of the bone when dividing the ribs for the gralloch.

In areas with regular severe winters a differentiation in cementum layers can be seen between the roots of the molars. It is very helpful to collect representative jawbones, prevail on an expert to cut and polish the molars in order to check the age by this method and so have a factual basis for a display of jawbones which will give a general indication of wear for age as it applies to that area. They should then be mounted on a board for reference.

The exterior of the carcass should be examined for any wounds and for parasites. Three of these are commonly encountered: the sheep tick (*Ixodes ricinus*) in its larval, nymph or adult forms, the latter usually attached firmly to the skin of the deer, the others after a short time to your own skin if they get a chance; the deer ked (*Lipoptena cervi*), which is a fairly large, free-moving insect in the coat, winged in September and subsequently wingless; and the biting louse (*Damalinia meyeri*), which is little thicker than a hair and is found in enormous quantities during the late winter on animals in poor condition. Lumps on the back may turn out to be larvae of the deer warble (*Hypoderma diana*), common on red deer in Scotland and occasionally on roe deer there. These large maggots are revolting and unsightly but they live in the tissue under the skin and the meat is not affected. At present deer warbles are unknown in England. Larvae of the nasal bot fly (*Cephenomyia stimulator*) may be found in the nasal cavities but this parasite, a major pest on the Continent, does not seem to be widespread among British roe.

The main internal parasites to look for are liver fluke (*Fasciola hepatica*), small leaf-shaped worms found curled up in the bile ducts which cause thickened or raised whitish areas on the liver, and lung worms (*Dictyocaulus spp.*), which are similar to those causing husk in cattle. Roe deer are rarely heard to cough, even when badly infested, but together with liver fluke these worms are probably one of the main natural population controls and a prime cause of heavy mortality where density has been allowed to become too high. The worms themselves are difficult to find in the air tubes of the lungs, but they set up a type of pneumonia which permanently scars the lungs with whitish areas, particularly at the edges. A high incidence of lung worms almost certainly means that the population is too high.

Roe as a whole are very healthy and they suffer from few diseases which are significant either to their own population dynamics or to the health of domestic stock. However, when gralloching an animal an eye should be kept open for anything unusual. Any abnormal lumps or growths should not be handled or cut open. Advice in the first place should be sought from a veterinary surgeon. The most common abnormality is to find the lungs or other internal organs adhering to the body wall, particularly the ribs. This can be the result of disease but it is more often the long-term effect of a road accident. The capacity of roe to survive after impact with a car is astonishing, but the long-term effects can often be traced in the form of broken limbs, malformed antlers and cracked ribs.

One important condition which can affect the stalker himself is Lyme Disease. Any tick bites which leave a spreading red mark should be viewed with suspicion. If the mark approaches the size of a 10p piece you should consult your GP, telling him you suspect Lyme Disease. Early treatment with antibiotics is effective but if neglected the disease can have serious long-term consequences.

The amount of internal fat around the kidneys and elsewhere gives an important index of condition which can be noted and each doe should be examined for signs of pregnancy. Later the presence and number of foetuses and their sex should be recorded.

Before burying or hiding the gralloch it is worthwhile opening up the rumen to see whether the contents can be identified so that you know what the animal was feeding on. All this information should be written down on the spot in the small notebook which all stalkers should carry.

Dogs for deer

Anyone doing much stalking should own and train a dog for the purpose unless town life makes it impossible. There is no difficulty in combining this work with game shooting. The basic obedience training is the same and a retriever or German pointer with the temperament to walk at heel, a soft mouth for birds and working ability will have no difficulty in deciding whether you are shooting game or stalking deer.

Our lack of comprehension of the world of scent in which roe live can be helped enormously by having a dog trained to walk at heel, to sit indefinitely on command and to find a deer after the shot. The companionship of a dog adds enormously to the pleasure of any stalking outing. Many different breeds are used for the purpose, from terriers to gundogs. The requirement is obedience

Snow makes it easy to recognise a blood trail. When the cover is thick, time and care is needed to find each spot.

and the possession of a nose. Small dogs are handy to take up high seats; larger breeds can catch and hold a lightly wounded roe until the owner comes up with it. The specialists in this field are the continental hunter-pointer-retriever (H.P.R.) breeds: pointers, Weimaraners, Munsterlanders and Vislas. An outing with one is an education. In thick cover many more deer will be spotted by attending closely to the dog's reactions to scent than would ever be possible unaided. One must remember, however, that the dog's nose only covers the upwind sector. Other segments of the circle need just as careful spying as ever. Remember that thin-coated breeds cannot be left sitting for long periods in cold weather, under a high seat for example, which would be nothing to a Labrador.

In addition to pointing live deer, the dog should be trained to follow the line of a wounded animal after the shot and to bark when it is brought to bay or found dead. Even with a mortal shot a deer may rush off 50 yards or more and in heavy cover may require a long search or even be lost without the services of a dog. Dogs can also be used to help in moving deer, providing they do not alarm them or chase them into running rather than walking when they pass the ambushed rifle.

Dog training for deer has been studied much more intensively on the Continent and various specialist breeds have been evolved which are used to follow a cold scent some hours after the deer has passed. They are not normally taken with the stalker or used on a hot scent.

We all try to make every shot a good one and not to do anything that will risk inflicting suffering on a deer. Your dog is your insurance policy but also the source of endless pleasure, companionship and satisfaction – especially when he finds a deer that someone else has wounded! Help in training a deer dog is available from specialists in this work.

A well-trained dog is the stalker's insurance policy.

Skinning and butchery

Introducing the notion of having your prized (and probably rather gory) deer cooked may call for diplomacy of a high order, especially if there have been any bad experiences in the past, say with shot-up pheasants, or a fish that wasn't quite the thing when it was produced. The whole trick is to produce your offerings to the kitchen in as near supermarket-wrapping state as is humanly possible. Between the moment of euphoria when you have finally taken a successful shot at a deer and the rowan jelly stage there is a lot of humping and dirty work to do. As a roe-stalker, it is very unlikely that anybody is going to do it for you, or even offer to help, so there is no alternative to learning how to make a decent job of it. Besides anything else, we owe it to the deer to make good use of everything edible, otherwise shooting it was a shame and a waste.

There is your beast, hanging in a cool, airy place like the garage. What's next? If it is a buck, take the head off immediately and soak it in a bucket of cold water until you have time to boil out the trophy. Do not attempt to skin the beast until it is time to cut it up, so that the joints can be packed for freezing or sent straight to the kitchen. Venison exposed to the air quickly goes black and hard on the surface.

Skinning is best done in two stages. First lay the carcass down on a clean surface and cut the skin from the central gralloch line up the inside of each leg. You can use your normal stalking knife, but it must be really sharp. If skinning seems to be getting slower and slower, stop and resharpen it. If you have a special blade with a thickened, blunt point, it slips under the skin without cutting into the meat. Start the peeling process away from each cut, pulling the skin and pushing at the junction with your other hand. The lower legs should be detached by disjointing – you will find the place just below where you think it is! Get someone to show you if you get

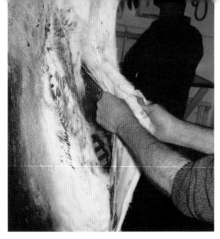

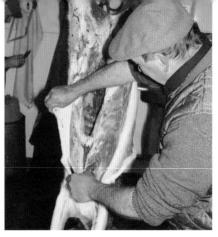

To skin – hang the carcass from two hooks to avoid swinging, cut up inside the legs and start to pull the skin away from the skirt.

Work towards the spine, only using the knife where pulling gets difficult.

the chance, or go to a B.D.S. stalkers' course, which is a very good idea anyway, and get it demonstrated. Next having made this start, hang the beast up at a convenient working height. Don't use a gambrel but support each haunch independently, otherwise it will twirl round while you are skinning and at a later stage fall on the floor.

Much can be done just with muscle-power, helped at difficult places with the knife to ease away the connecting tissue. Try to work from the belly towards the backbone, then forwards to the neck. Cut the head off close behind the skull. Pick off as many loose hairs as you can, and you are ready for jointing. Lay some

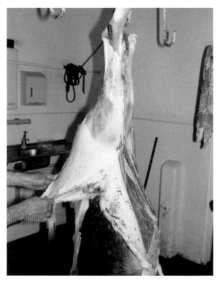

Pull the skin down over the haunches, taking care not to tear the meat.

Start the cutting process by separating the forelegs. They are only attached by muscle.

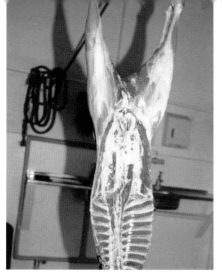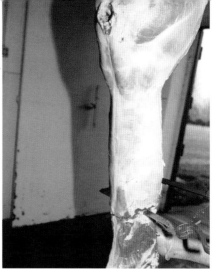

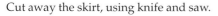

Cut away the skirt, using knife and saw.   Cut off the neck, leaving ten ribs on the saddle.

polythene on a table so that everything can be kept clean, cut off and discard any damaged or bloodshot meat and then cut off the two shoulders. Unlike ourselves, deer do not have a collarbone, so by pulling outwards, the job can be done neatly with a knife alone. Lay the shoulders on the polythene. Then cut the neck off close to the shoulders and saw off the ribs just outside of the fillets which run each side of the backbone. The two haunches need to be divided at this point, sawing carefully between them down to where the loin (saddle) begins. If you cut the saddle off first there is nothing to steady when you are sawing.

Then cut one haunch away from the saddle. That's when everything falls on the floor if you haven't supported both haunches independently! Cut off the other, and put the saddle on the table.

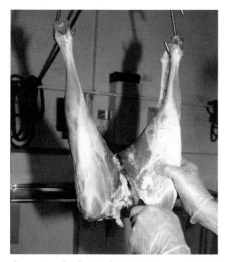

Finally shorten the haunches to save freezer room by detaching the shanks. A knife inserted in the white area at the 'knee' will disjoint it neatly.

Separate the haunches.

Both haunches are now hanging free and can be taken down safely.

The Good Venison Guide

- Ask how the cook wants the meat presented.
- Everything clean, not hairy or bloodstained.
- Freeze or cook immediately after skinning.
- Label bags with felt-tip: date, age, sex, species, contents.

Now for the fine work! Find out from the Master Cook how he or she wants the joints presented: the saddle entire or as two fillets; the haunches and shoulders as roasting joints or boned out. This is going to be a professional job. Start with the haunches by shortening them: poke a knife into the white area at the 'knee' and wiggle it about until the joint gives way, detach the shank and it leaves a handy oven-ready joint finishing at the hamstring. Bag, seal and label them (a broad felt-tip does well) with age, sex, date shot and 'haunch', then put them in the coldest part of the freezer while you get on with the rest. The saddle makes a wonderfully flavoursome joint cooked on the bone (it's the only bit of a roe which benefits from undercooking), but otherwise run your knife on either side of the backbone to make two long strips of the very best meat, for cooking as such, or dividing into steaks. In either case the whitish sinew needs to be removed from the surface. Detach a tab of it, take a firm grip with a pair of pliers and pull the whole thing past a knife, leaving a thick red fillet of meat and an elastic length of sinew. Practice makes perfect, but it is worth the effort. Bag and label as before.

I personally prefer to bone the shoulders. Often there is some damage from the shot, and it is a poor joint to roast. Chase out the shoulder-blade and leg bone and then dice what is left into stew meat, carefully removing all fragments of sinew, with which the shoulder is all too well supplied. Bag in measured 1 lb or 2 lb lots, labelled accordingly. I said it would be a professional job! The neck of a doe hasn't much meat on it, but some can be boned out and added to the stew meat, or you can saw it into sections when it can be treated like oxtail and cooked off the bone. All you are left with are the ribs, which frankly are not much of an asset. They can always be boiled up with the other bones for stock, or for your deserving dog.

Carefully wash and sterilise the meat saw and knife, clean up and wash down. That's the best way to get full domestic approval when the next chance of a stalking trip comes up, not to speak of sitting down to that succulent roast venison!

Trophies – preparation and measurement

Mugging up on the subject of boiling out a head before you actually have one seems a bit like tempting Murphy to apply his Law. However, in the wild excitement of finally achieving the longed-for buck there is quite a lot to do which needs fairly prompt action if you are going to have something on the wall to be proud of. One vital decision has to be made just as soon as an exceptional buck has been shot: will there be any question of having the head fully mounted (stuffed)? If so, great care must be taken not to cut the skin up the throat. The taxidermist will need as much skin as he can have, so cut round *behind* the shoulders and along the line of the back to the start of the neck. The neck is skinned as a tube up to the back of the skull, which is detached with all this skin attached. Do not treat the head or skin with anything, but roll it up and freeze it as soon as ever you can. Then you can contact a taxidermist at leisure. If the hair is shedding, as is often the case in spring, it is not disastrous. A second buck's skin shot later in the summer can be tailored to fit.

What You Will Need

- Your stalking knife
- A strong blunt scraping knife
- A backless wood saw
- A pair of strong electrician's bent-nosed pliers
- Washing soda crystals
- Household hydrogen peroxide (20 vol)
- Cotton wool
- A non-aluminium saucepan dedicated to head-boiling
- Camping-Gaz or other heat source not in the kitchen
- A wooden shield, home-made or bought, and a 25 mm×8 wood-screw (cut skull) or 60 mm×8 (full skull)

Boiling out a trophy
Most stalkers like to preserve their roe trophies by cleaning and bleaching the skull, leaving the antlers in their original colour, without coating them with varnish, which looks dreadful, or artificially polishing the points.

Having decided that you want this trophy on the wall as a skull and antlers, the first thing is to cut off the buck's head close behind the ears as soon as you get home. Cut the skin round with a knife, then use a saw unless you have been shown how to disconnect the top vertebra. While you deal with the carcass, stick the head in a bucket of

Put the head in a bucket of cold water as soon as possible.

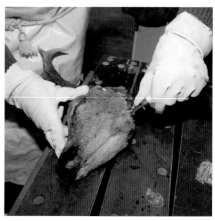

Rough skin the head, starting under the jaw.

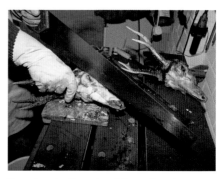

Continue skinning up to the pedicles, taking care not to score the frontal bone.

Lay the skull on its side and make a cut according to the diagram. If the cut wanders, turn over and start on the other side rather than trying to force the saw.

Using a skull-cutting jig. This stalker has adapted an electric jigsaw for the purpose.

Boil in a non-aluminium pan with soda in the water for about twenty minutes, depending on age.

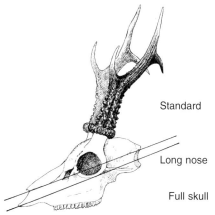

Standard

Long nose

Full skull

The standard and long-nose cuts for roe trophies.

Once the skull has been scraped clean after boiling, coat the bone with cotton wool and soak it with hydrogen peroxide for up to twelve hours. It will dry out clean and white.

cold water. This will start to clean it and prevent staining. It will stay there happily for up to twenty-four hours, although in hot weather you will need to change the water periodically.

Put the head on a workbench and roughly skin it, working from the jaw upwards. Scratches on the frontal bone will show for ever. Run the knife inside the jawbones to release the tongue and cut the muscles which attach the jaw to the skull. Cut off the tongue (there is usually a dog waiting below at this point) and pull the jaw down and back until it hinges away. Help by cutting attachments as it comes.

Unless you are going to mount the whole skull, put the skull sideways on the bench with a block under the nose and saw off what you don't need. Use a wood saw, not a meat saw, as they don't cut straight. Some stalkers cut through the eye socket, others leave a 'long-nose' which just removes the upper teeth leaving the two oval nose bones on the trophy. Saw halfway through, then see if you are going straight. If not, start again from the other side, so that the botch is unseen in the middle, not a wild sawcut up one side!

Immerse the skull in boiling water up to, but not including, the coronets. You may need to secure the head somehow to achieve this, and the water will need topping up to keep it just right. Put about 50 g of washing soda in the water. Don't use an aluminium pot, as the soda will attack it, and don't boil heads in the kitchen – if you want to avoid extreme adverse reactions to deer

ROE DEER: MANAGEMENT AND STALKING

stalking from the family! A young roe buck may be ready in fifteen minutes, an old one probably needs half an hour. Don't let it boil dry! The smell is appalling.

When the flesh starts to peel away from the bone, take it out and with your knife and the pliers scrape all tissue away from the bone, and the brain and fine nasal structures from inside the skull. An expert can do a cut skull in little more than quarter of an hour. You will take longer the first time. It has to be done well. A strong jet of water helps to empty the nose and brain cavities.

While the skull is still damp, wrap it in a thin layer of cotton wool (kitchen paper towel will do, but isn't so good) put a wad in each eye socket and inside the brain pan. Keep it clear of the coronets, or they will be bleached. Then pour on hydrogen peroxide, which will degrease and whiten the bone. Don't use the strong sort, or chlorine bleach. Wash any splashes off your hands or the antlers themselves. In an hour or two your trophy will be ready to wash under a tap and put to dry. An old buck's skull can be left overnight.

Bore a hole in the shield to coincide with the bridge of bone between the eye sockets and screw the skull to it from the back. Screw heads showing in front look awful. If it is a home-made shield, buy a brass glass plate so that it can hang up neatly where you can be proud of it.

Measuring length.

Measuring trophies

A simple way of recording the details of the bucks you shoot was shown on page 63. If you shoot a big one, then you will want to know how it measures up against a national or international scale and this can be done by using the formula developed by the Conseil International de la Chasse (C.I.C.) for judging trophies at trophy shows abroad. International shows are largely a thing of the past,

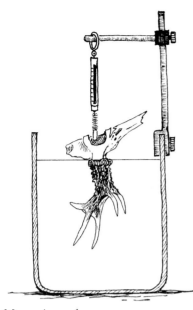
Measuring volume.

but now you can have a trophy measured by the C.I.C.'s U.K. Trophy Commission (addresses are in Appendix 4). The actual process of measurement has to follow strict rules and involves calculating the volume of the antlers by immersing them in water without wetting the skull. Certain features are awarded beauty points. The form used is shown in the box on page 134. Allowances are made according to how the skull has been cut. Medals are awarded for trophies reaching a certain standard.

With a reasonably accurate spring balance and a thin metal tape you can assess your own trophies by following the C.I.C. formula:

1. **Length** in centimetres, taken up the outside of the antlers from the bottom line of the coronet, following the curves to the top. Both antlers are measured and the average worked out. The points scored are the result of halving this average.
2. **Weight** of the antlers and skull in grams, cut through the eye sockets. If the whole skull without the lower jaw is retained 90 g is deducted, other cuts pro rata. Divide the net weight by ten to get the points scored.
3. **Volume.** Hang the head from a spring balance with the antlers downwards and immerse them in water to the bottom of the coronets. No part of the pedicles may be submerged. The antlers must of course be hanging free in the water. Record the weight in grams as shown by the spring balance when it is held thus and deduct it from the total dry weight of the skull and antlers. The resulting figure is divided by ten and multiplied by three to get the number of points.
4. **Span** measured at the widest part between the beams, expressed as a percentage of the average length. Points scored as follows:
   - less than 30 per cent nil
   - 30–34.9 per cent one point
   - 35–39.9 per cent two points
   - 40–44.9 per cent three points
   - 45–75 per cent four points
   - over 75 per cent nil.
5. **Colour.** Maximum four points for black, shading down to nil for white. Any artificial colouring, nil.

C.I.C. measurement Form

ROE BUCK

			Factor	Points
1 Antler length	Left 23.8 cm. Right 24.0 cm Total 47.8	Average 23.9	X 0.5	11.95
2 Weight	482 gm. Deduct 50 gm. Nett wt. 432 gm		X 0.1	43.2
3 Volume	Weight in air 482 gm **Weight in water 316 gm** Volume 166 cm³		X 0.3	49.8
4 Spread	Spread 11.3 cm X 100 = 47.2 % Av. Length 23.9 cm			4.0
5 Colour	Max points = 4			2.5
6 Pearling	Max points = 4			2.0
7 Coronets	Max points = 4			3.0
8 Tine Ends	Max points = 2			2.0
9 Additions	Max points = 5			3.0
	Total for 1 – 9			121.45
10 Deductions	Max points = 5			
	TOTAL SCORE			121.45

(Silver medal

6. **Pearling.** Small or none, nil; weak pearling one point; medium (many small pearls) two points; well-pearled (small pearls on all sides) three points; very good pearls (strong pearling on all sides, continued high on the beam) four points.

7. **Coronets.** Up to four points for development. They should be thick, rough and well-developed all round.

8. **Tine ends.** Two points maximum for sharp well-polished points down to nil for blunt, dull ones.

9. **Additions.** Up to five points for regularity and quality of tines, of which three points are reserved for regularity, and up to two points for their quality.

10. **Deductions.** Up to five points can be deducted, of which up to three are for unspecified abnormalities and up to two for missing or poor-quality tines.

To get some idea of whether your buck is heavy enough to merit having it judged, you can use this yardstick:

Skull weight* (uncut less lower jaw)	Skull weight* (cut)	Possible medal level**
455 g	365 g	Bronze
510 g	420 g	Silver
540 g	450 g	Gold

* Weight dry. Heads can only be judged three months after boiling.
** This is only a guide. Much depends on other factors, such as length, volume, regularity etc.

Score (C.I.C. points)	Medal
105 – 114.9 points	Bronze
115 – 129.9 points	Silver
130 points upwards	Gold

The Official record for a British roe head is 210.25 points, scored by a buck shot in Sussex in 1971 by Michael J. Langmead. The unofficial record for Scotland is 206.2 points, a buck shot in 1993 by C. E. van der Straten Waillet in Fife. A buck from Hampshire which was unofficially scored at 238.55 points was shot by Major the Hon. Peter Baillie in 1974. This trophy might have been taken for a perruque but in fact the antlers were normal, though massive and slightly porous. The skull was, however, grossly thickened. In consequence the buck was classified, quite rightly, as a freak and

Weighing the skull.

the score disallowed. Other bucks have been shot or found with similar thickening of the pedicles and skull. Among the largest was a buck which scored 236.25 points, shot in 1991 by Mr J. Pilkington in Wiltshire.

Roe were at one time introduced to Ireland. A colony existed at Lissadell, Co. Sligo from the 1860s and some exceptional heads were recorded. They were exterminated some time before the Second World War. Some trophies have survived. The best of these is a massive twelve-pointer which in the opinion of Kenneth Whitehead might score over 200 points. As the head is fully mounted it cannot be measured. The longest regular head from Britain measured by the Trophy Commission was a buck from Sussex shot by Mr de Buday Goldberger in 1968. It scored 156.3 points and had an antler length of 33.34 cm (13 in).

This fine gold-medal buck from Angus scored 146.5 points. *(Photo A Allison)*

PART 7

The Stalker's Year

Unlike many sports, roe stalking occupies the whole year. Each month has something to enjoy, something to do or see. This part of the book offers a little informal colour and a few tips month by month to clothe the bare bones of roe knowledge and stalking technique.

March

> **Hints for the Month**
> ***
> * Upgrade kids to yearlings on 1 March – it saves confusion with this year's crop.
> * Census work.
> * Decide on your buck cull.
> * Rifle maintenance and zeroing.
> * Check high seats.

Regardless of the calendar, March is the beginning of the deer year, the necessary starting point in the roe deer's annual round of fawning and rut, antler growth and fraying, summer territoriality and winter survival. The deer manager completes his records for the past season and makes plans for the next. In order to avoid confusion, he counts all his deer as one year older on 1 March, so that yesterday's kids are today's yearlings. It is also a busy month of preparation for the coming open season on bucks.

Roe deer are small, secretive beasts, possessed of a very fine set of senses and a brain quite capable of interpreting our actions to their own advantage. What have we roe stalkers to offer to measure up to them or even swing the balance occasionally in our favour? Not much, to be honest: eyes tired and myopic at the end of a week's staring at a V.D.U.; a poor nose – 'Even the scent of roses is not what we supposes'; worst of all, a dreadful sense of not wanting to waste time which urges the weekend stalker to dash through the woods from one supposed hot spot to another instead of pausing in the first long enough for a buck to appear in the course of his leisured morning patrol. Patience is a virtue which does not come easily in these days of commercial pressures.

Because March is – or should be – a month when roe of either sex are left unshot, an enthusiastic stalker can make very good use of his time in quiet observation of the deer on his ground. No rifle – no point in hurrying. The time spent will pay a heavy dividend later when the buck season opens. Family groups will still be seen, so one can get a good idea of the previous year's breeding success. Just note down the number of mature does and the number of yearlings (kids of the previous summer) as you look into successive feeding grounds. It is important data for deciding the number of yearling bucks to take next month and eventually in planning the doe cull.

With no hurried decisions to make about sex, status and safety before taking a shot, just watch the deer quietly and you will begin to notice aspects of the day-to-day life which helps you to understand them and increases the prospects of a good success rate through the months to come.

At this time of year you will see that the individuals in so-called 'family' groups often change. In fact there is increasing turbulence in most roe populations just now. The more forward yearling bucks are tending to drift away from their mothers, turning briefly to an older buck to learn survival technique from him before he becomes morose and aggressive with the arrival of the territorial phase and boots the youngster out to go wandering. As fawning time gets nearer the does themselves get intolerant of their previous year's offspring, even the females, and can be seen chasing them off with flattened ears and flailing forelegs. As an individualistic rather than a herding species, it's all part of the roe's inbuilt drive to emigrate rather than allow the population to rise above the capacity of the habitat to support them.

Sometimes in early spring herds of twenty or more roe can be seen in the fields, which seems to go against this aspect of their behaviour. This may just indicate that there is a particularly succulent crop which attracts them, but otherwise this 'field roe behaviour' only occurs in areas where the fields are comparatively large, where the available cover is overused and where the roe population has been allowed to get too high. If a little investigation shows this to be true, then remedial action should form part of the management plans you make for the coming year. These bands tend to break up as the farm crops get higher and more leaves flush in the woods, but under normal circumstances in this country the field roe phenomenon ought to be regarded as an indicator of problems needing to be faced.

While any attempts to count the actual number of roe on your stalking are too inaccurate to be worthwhile, these sessions of pure observation in March and early April will at least indicate a minimum figure. If the landlord, farm staff and gamekeeper are agreeable it is worth reinforcing this with a few night expeditions round the fields with a powerful spotlight. You may be surprised! Any indication you can get of a trend – upwards or downwards – in numbers seen from one year to another, and the proportion of bucks to does observed is more significant in practical deer management than a theoretical population figure. Did you shoot enough does last winter? Did you take too many mature bucks? A balanced population with enough natural food to eat is less likely to land you in trouble because of unreasonable damage to trees or crops. On low-ground and south-country areas the amount of bramble and ivy left within reach at the end of winter should be noted.

At the same time there is no harm in looking forward to the coming season and checking over your high seats. Are they sound? Your responsibilities in this direction are serious under the Health and Safety Regulations (see Appendix 6), not only to yourself and your guests but to the general public – invited or otherwise! Wooden seats, especially those made of untreated wood, rot with horrifying speed and become highly dangerous in consequence. Even treated ones tend to go at ground level and need checking regularly. Are they in the right place, or has the plantation they were meant to protect grown up so that deer would be invisible? Usually there is a useful job of pruning to be done, opening up the

Before the buck season, get to know your ground and the way the deer use it.

While the deer are using the fields, see how many kids per doe have survived the winter and assess the sex ratio of mature animals.

arcs of fire for those in the right place, while outgrown seats should be shifted to better sites or demolished if they are past moving. Metal seats may need repainting and checking over. Plastic chair-seats may have become brittle after long exposure. Make sure that the rope securing a lean-to seat to its tree is not chafed. Any double seats which you plan to occupy with a visitor in the buck season need particular attention. Stalkers on the whole tend to be lean and fit, but that does not necessarily apply to their guests. High seats must comply with standards set down and must be maintained in a safe state.

April

Hints for the Month

- Remind those concerned that you will be out morning and evening.
- Make a good start on the yearling buck cull.
- Locate and identify territorial bucks.
- Practise informal shooting positions until you are comfortable and steady.
- If you stalk in remote areas, take a mobile phone. Accidents can happen.

Every stalker longs to be out in the woods on the first day: everything is chock-full of excitement and promise. Maybe you have been able to spend some time spying out the ground beforehand, locating promising bucks, seeing which rides are passable and if forestry work has opened up any useful clearings. Certainly there must have been the chance of a few shots to restore confidence in the rifle's zero. It is going to be an early start, when the brain doesn't react too quickly and in the hurry of getting off something can so easily be forgotten. To save time all your gear needs to be laid out the night before – clothes, boots, stalking jacket, hat. For security one cannot take the rifle or ammo out of the gunsafe, but a case laid with the rest reminds you that these items need to be taken out first thing. Don't forget the bolt!

One doesn't sleep much before the opening day: I have jumped out of bed in a panic before now and been half into my stalking gear before I realised that it was still bright moonlight! Who wouldn't make an early start anyway on such a morning? But not with three or four hours of the night still to go. If you are lucky and able to spend the night near your stalking ground it is possible to judge the time to issue out as a welcome cup of coffee gets the pulse going. It is always brighter outside than it looks from a lighted room: the slightest hint of midnight blue replaces black night and it is time to be shifting. Once outside, the birds are singing and there is that wonderful smell of spring in the air besides your own sense of adventure. A pheasant crows in the woods and you are off!

Pat your pockets to make sure that all the essentials are in: knife, ammo, binoculars, rifle, bolt, scope, stick, roe sack, car keys. I used to stay in a pub in Wiltshire where they didn't mind our going out early provided we posted the massive front door key back through the letter-box. That really made one check for the vitals – you couldn't even go back to bed if something essential had been left behind. The best thing is to keep a postcard handy

with a list of essentials (one suggestion is to be found on page 91). Of course if you are one of those photographic memory people, you do not need it, but I do – especially at 4.30 a.m! Some of the things are seasonal, like calls and insect cream, and a lot of small things lurk in the roe sack pockets until needed.

It is wonderful to feel that you have the countryside to yourself at that hour of the morning, but don't bet on it. Odd characters tend to wander about at all hours these days – often where they have no

Each newly used fraying stock indicates the presence of a buck.

right to be – so be careful before you shoot, no matter what the temptation. Because of the numbers of folk about, go easy on the Rambo stuff – big sheath knives and disruptive-pattern jackets give a false impression. Anything soft in finish and drab green or brown is just as good. Remember that deer are more or less colour-blind; it is movement that they are so quick to spot.

I certainly get more pleasure out of a good pair of binoculars than anything; they open the woodland book to anyone who goes slowly enough to use them to identify and watch anything that catches the eye – bird and beast besides the deer – and going slowly is the essence of woodland stalking. In the States they call it still-hunting, which is very telling. Have the glasses on a short but wide strap round your neck ready for use.

In the excitement of early dawn it is easy to move off too fast when the flat light makes animals difficult to spot. Yes, an old, old buck may play safe by retiring into cover pretty soon after dawn, but this is the first day of a new season and even he will be a little less wary than is the case a few weeks hence. Until the sun comes up you will be looking for silhouettes – the Vee–shape of a pair of enquiring ears; the horizontal line of a back, maybe a flash of white from a roe target if you are lucky. In this half-light anything suspicious needs to be examined carefully with the binoculars steadied on your stalking stick. Nine times out of ten it will be some innocent object, even a cock pheasant or a hare moving slowly in the undergrowth, but the tenth just may be the buck of your dreams!

Sooner or later the incredible moment comes and *there one is*! Don't panic, throw yourself flat, grab the rifle or do anything else quickly. Fast movement will give you away instantly, and if a deer has seen you already the best thing may well be to stand still

As the bucks grow their full heads and start to fray, try to keep notes of them, estimating age and noting the length and number of points. *(Photo R Bowles)*

regardless of your position until he has relaxed. This may take what seems an age and if it catches you on one leg, it can be agonising. A careful look through the glasses is always the first rule when a roe does give itself away. Is it a buck or a doe? Young or old? Is it a safe shot? What were your instructions about selection? All these things need to be decided before there is any thought of letting the glass go and reaching for the rifle. Then the great question is – dare I move a muscle? Maybe it has seen you but is not seriously alarmed. There may be a show of head-jerking, a pretence of eating or even a few nervous steps. Even then it is better to keep your nerve, no matter how heart-stopping the moment. There is a good chance that the buck will relax if you remain completely motion-less and then the gradual hand movements can start. Your heart may stop pounding too.

Once the beast has relaxed, or if you weren't noticed to start with, inch the binoculars up to have a careful look – first to see if you think it shootable, and then to check for any twigs in the way of the bullet, and whether there is a solid butt of earth behind. *A background of trees is not sufficient as a bullet stop.*

Now the big question is 'Should I shoot?' That probably won't need much decision if it is your very first buck and it is the open season. However, very soon after that stage every stalker needs to think a bit about what he is trying to do and how to go about it. If you have studied the section on management you will be in a better position to make that vital decision.

May

> **Hints for the Month**
> ---
> - Use a rifle cover and conceal the rifle, bolt removed, when it is in the car.
> - Stop somewhere on the way, test the wind and plan your stalk accordingly. Plans made overnight rarely work.
> - *Still-hunting* is the word. You may feel tempted to go quick-ly from one 'good place' to the next. Trophy bucks live to be old by living in unexpected corners.

Being out in the dawn woods just as the blue night pales is magical in itself. In the summer it is the peak hour for birdsong, but while taking in the surroundings and enjoying them, success in stalking a deer means the most intense concentration on that alone. From the moment you shut the car door – and it must be done with the least noise for alien sounds will alert deer for hundreds of yards – your attention must be totally concentrated on your environment, ears, eyes and that indefinable sense which really does warn you if a deer is about. A state of unity with the life of the wood can only be achieved by intense concentration and unbelievably slow progress. There is always a strong inclination to hurry towards some good spot, perhaps where you saw a deer previously, and it is perhaps the most difficult lesson of all to fix in your mind that once in the wood, you are just as likely to see a deer where you are as where you intended to go.

If you move like a shadow, if you are tuned to your surroundings, nature will tell you what is about. Everyone knows, for example, that blackbirds have an alarm note when they locate an owl, but how many realise that they have a different call which reveals a deer? Move quickly and even if you don't break the occasional stick, your two-footed tread in the leaves will alert every beast within hearing. You know how difficult it is to stalk a roosting woodpigeon, but put one or two of them off during a stalk and their clattering flight will reveal your progress quite sufficiently to make feeding deer melt into the undergrowth.

Modern life teaches us to hurry, to 'go for it'. Success in woodland stalking is much more likely to come from sitting on a log for half a hour at a time than traipsing round the woods alerting everything to the idea that a predator is about, and what is worse, teaching them when you are likely to be stalking and the routes you prefer. Remember this: deer are not fools, and if we choose to study them occasionally, they study us as if their lives depend on it – as of course they do.

Although the buck season opens on 1 April the weather is often

As the cover thickens you will have to go slower and look harder to spot the deer. *(Photo J Poutsma)*

cold and wet, nor will all the major bucks be completely clear of velvet. The month should have been mainly devoted to attending to the yearling cull, locating major bucks' territories and becoming generally familiarised with your ground. Crops and forest operations may have made profound changes which will be reflected in the habits of the deer. By May, the traditional opening of the roe buck season, one should be able to go out full of enthusiasm, but with the knowledge which will allow you to take full advantage of the few precious weeks before leaf flush and bracken growth make spotting your deer really difficult.

In woodland one stalks with a loaded rifle, on safe and slung from the shoulder, so one has to be extra careful. The safety catch can get brushed off, so check it regularly. If you use a stick, and I find one an enormous help in the woods, study the advice on page 94 and get used to the feeling of slinging the rifle on your right shoulder, muzzle down, with the stick in the left. If you are worried about the possibility of mud or snow blocking the end of the barrel, stick some plastic tape over the muzzle – it is quite safe with a rifle. When the great chance comes may St Hubert and all the kind gods of stalking steady your jumping nerves and direct your aim – and there he will lie: the first mature buck of the season!

June

Midsummer abundance can pose real problems for the woodland stalker after the excitements of the opening weeks of the buck season, even to the point of discouraging all but the most keen. The nights, especially in the north, are brief to vanishing point and one can get tired to death after a few days' stalking. The bucks which

Deer late in shedding their winter coat or late in cleaning their antlers may be ill and need a second look. *(Photo J Poutsma)*

you had pinpointed in May have sunk into a sea of greenery; even from a high seat the most one can hope to see are antler tips or flicking ears. Remember that it just is not worth trying to estimate where the body might be – it won't! And bullets behave unpredictably when fired through vegetation, even a thin cereal crop.

Hints for the Month

- When trying to assess the age of a roe, study the line of back and backside: sharp angles at pinbone and tail indicate young beasts, rounded outlines suggest maturity.
- Bucks still in winter coat or in velvet may be ill, old or in poor condition.
- Nights are very short. Get enough sleep during the day or your stalking and shooting ability will suffer.
- If you feel sleepy when driving – *stop*. Five minutes' kip will do everything for your safety.

However, all is not lost. If your stalking includes any fields, the deer may be coming on to them early and late either to get a change of food or to escape the flies. For a time the crops will be low enough to allow the rather specialised sport of tramline hunting. Tramlines are the double wheelmarks left by successive sprayer passes through the crop. Deer use them, and so can the stalker! It is a curious thing that when deer are in cover low enough to expose the line of the back, they often get the idea that they cannot be seen and permit liberties to be taken. Having located a shootable beast, perhaps in the middle of 70 acres of oilseed rape or wheat, you choose a tramline which will take you in range, hustle down it crouched double, pop up at the critical point and go bang. It sounds easy – only the popping up at the right moment and not before can be tricky. At all events it can be fun and quite rewarding until the crop gets that bit higher and hides the deer altogether. A two-piece stick is very handy to make a tall bipod and give a steady shot over high cover.

Having said that, if one is trying to make a decent job of deer management the best time of the year is over. The necessary cull of yearlings should be collected while they are still in their family groups during April. After that the bucks start to chase them about and in efforts to get a territory they start fraying. An accumulation of yearlings in a new plantation can produce a frightening amount of fraying and your name will be mud with the owner and his forester. By the beginning of the month if your

The long model bipod gives better chances of a steady sitting shot over tall grasses.

stalking happens to be first-class roe habitat the majority of the yearlings will have been evicted from the best places, leaving only adult bucks with a few non-aggressive stragglers. You will have lost the best chance of getting near your cull target for yearlings. Other stalkers with less desirable conditions may be on the receiving end of emigration and will not thank their more fortunate neighbours for discharging a torrent of yearlings onto their ground where they will have to be shot in the much more difficult conditions of midsummer and beyond.

Getting any ride mowing done now the vegetation is at its height is always a problem. Farm tractors are frantic with silaging and other urgent work, gamekeepers are at full stretch with rearing and promises tend to come to nothing. In any case one doesn't want to cut more than the centre strip of a broad ride and destroy herbs and low growth which are needed as cover for ground-nesting birds and as food for various butterflies. That work is better done later in the year. Where bracken grows everywhere, it is worth discussing the idea of spraying small areas with the selective herbicide Asulox, choosing places which are well used by the deer and which can be overlooked either from natural viewpoints or high seats. Spraying is expensive but if the application is timed right very little bracken will grow up the next season and the effect will probably last for several years. In other areas, depending on the underlying soil, certain places may be relatively or completely bracken-free and a strategically placed high seat there will be useful all through the summer. Larch plantations are particularly useful because there should be enough light to allow bramble to grow underneath. It is thinned early so one can often erect a high seat in a fifteen-year-old larch block, knowing that it stands in a roe larder and will be usable for years ahead. All that is needed is a path from any convenient access point kept clear of the inevitable crackly twigs.

Farther north one can depend on at least some roe using the boundary area between forest and hill. An evening's stalk along the top fence of any typical hillside conifer block can be rewarding and may disclose quite a few otherwise reclusive bucks drifting upwards from their usual haunts, presumably to get a breath of cooler wind or relief from the flies. From time to time I have encountered roe that lived way out in the heather, and those not the fugitive yearlings I expected. Though they may see very few people in the year, or perhaps because of it, these hill-living deer are often extremely shy, appearing to use their eyesight much more than totally woodland animals. Stalking them can be a real challenge as they have to be approached with the same technique as hill red deer and when disturbed they do not dodge behind the nearest knoll before relaxing but once out of sight take to their heels and all one sees is a series of bobbing white backsides in the far distance.

July

Hints for the Month

- Practise your calls – but not in the woods!
- Don't call until the rut is well on.
- In hill country roe often go up to escape the flies.
- Recently harvested fields may reveal roe which have been living unseen in the fields all summer.

Although in the height of summer the cover is at its thickest and flies and midges make life for the stalker a burden on muggy evenings, the roe rut promises great things. As July comes round in the roe-stalking year, it is not only the deer who get rutting fever! We are all in a ferment to detect the first signs of activity. Calls get sorted out and face veils unearthed from where they were left last summer, and we launch out with renewed keenness into what an ex-R.A.F. friend refers to as a Maximum Effort. Usually we are all far too early, and the effort falls off for lack of success or the demands of watering the garden. This is all too often just as the rut really gets going; the first doe comes visibly into season, calling comes finally into its own and the steamy or baking days are full of roe activity.

A fatal encounter. Fighting, though infrequent, can be savage. These two bucks got their antlers meshed.

Various whistles made to imitate the squeaks of an in-season roe doe are available from gunshops and stalking specialists. You can also get an audio cassette demonstrating how to call. Calls which you just have to blow are the easiest to use; another type has an external reed, which needs quite a bit of practice to get right but can bring bucks in when the others fail.

Even early in July if the weather is warm you will see the first stirring of the rut. Make a mental note of the location of such early birds as they are quite likely to be the older bucks, but do not attempt to use a call. Calling is mostly only effective when there is a doe actually in season somewhere locally – the bucks know their pheromones! The rut proper will probably not get going until late in the month, lasting into August. Practising on a call only educates roe in yet another of man's wiles. By all means get out what calls you have, make sure the dust is blown out of them and that the reeds are in good condition. Trial peeping in the woods is inadvisable. At home it makes the dogs bark and may evoke a prompt and angry response from those trying to do homework or watch the telly. That leaves the car for your studio, but make sure the windows are closed unless you want to get arrested! There will be plenty of time for calling after you have seen serious chasing or attempted mating.

Early in the rut, the doe is very particular about the partner she is prepared to accept as a suitor. Equally, she is very jealous of any attempt he may make to wander off and philander. This means that where the sex ratio is reasonably level, calling can be very unrewarding until mating has actually taken place. Curiously enough, after that a free-for-all can develop where bucks may be seen mating with several different does who appear to be equally promiscuous. It may be a provision of nature to ensure the maximum number of does are safely pregnant at the end of their one annual heat. At all events, these are the conditions when suddenly calling is easy and bucks appear from all directions. I once called a buck right in close for a Women's Institute party, all in cotton frocks. He must have been short-sighted – or desperate!

While it may be frustrating for anyone just keen to let off his rifle, watching the deer is fascinating as the process of courtship develops. The rigid territory system of spring and early summer starts to break down and familiar males may be seen in surprising places, or questing bucks may turn up that are complete strangers. Whether they really have come from over the boundary or were there all the time is a matter for speculation.

Part of this early-rut mobility may be due to the essentially selective attitude of the doe when she accepts or rejects a buck as her mate. It is so difficult for us to understand the complicated relationship between a buck and a doe occupying more or less the same ground. While they are doubtless aware of one another's movements, at no time does this liaison resemble pair behaviour as one gets in birds, for example. As the rut approaches the buck may start to make overtures to the doe who for reasons closed to us fails to be impressed. Up to the time of the first mating she seems to be extremely particular about choosing a consort and examples are on record among marked roe of females leaving their own territory for what one could describe as a round of visits to neighbouring chaps, as if none of them quite measured up to her demanding standards, or as if her morals were on the relaxed side in our terms.

Similarly the bucks, deprived of does which previously accepted their presence, break well-established 'gentlemen's agreements' and start searching for a mate over a wider radius. Added to them are the ever-hopeful non-territorial males which have been excluded from the best ground since last spring.

Acceptance of one male by the doe seems to start with a series of high-speed chases, as one often sees in the early stages of the rut. I suspect that this is not so much a test of his stamina as a gradual process of breaking down the doe's reluctance to be touched at all by another beast. Unlike cattle, roe are non-contact animals. Once the bond has been broken between mother and young at the end of the winter, or between siblings which may persist a little longer in the form of mutual grooming, roe do not normally touch one another, and even under the mating drive this reluctance may need time to break.

By late summer the kids' spots are fading. One will be able to see them until the first winter coat grows through.

Nearer to mating, the tempo slows and one may see the buck either closely following, nose outstretched, or pressing his chin on the doe's rump. Mating is likely to come shortly after, sometimes after a series of unsuccessful attempts on the buck's part. Once mated for the first time that year, the doe's attitude seems to change profoundly, and she may accept other bucks without much apparent discrimination.

The onset of the rut varies widely between years and from one part of the country to another. To judge by stalkers' conversations at successive Game Fairs, much depends on the weather. A hot July brings it forward while a miserable wet spell can apparently shut down any rutting activity or delay it by a week or more. When we have had really bad summers there has been no lack of kids the following spring, so I assume from this that courtship is either cut down to a minimum, or takes place at night. There is no doubt that the best conditions for calling are when it is windless (maybe just because the noise carries better) and when the temperature is fairly high. Rain or shine is possibly less significant. During the exceptional summer of 1995 it just seemed too hot during the day, and calling in general was more productive early morning and late evening, which certainly is not the case in normal years.

Before the deer really start to move and bark aggressively, stalking can be very difficult. If you do get the chance of a shot, try to put the animal down on the spot, otherwise finding it quickly enough may be difficult. Watch carefully the behaviour of the beast, and be sure to mark with extra care where it was standing. A buck in rut always has more stamina than usual, and a fatal shot may still result in the beast running fifty or a hundred yards before falling. Take note of the direction he takes and listen like mad for a crash which indicates where he has fallen.

August

Bringing a buck to the call can be breathtakingly exciting – the summit of stalking skill and of the year for many roe enthusiasts. It is a combination of real woodcraft, mastery of calling technique and a real understanding of roe behaviour. Success may be marked by a crashing approach, a silent, cunning circling of the caller by a suspicious buck or even a slow, ambling appearance as if the buck just happened to be coming that way. Either way, make no mistake – he knows what is on!

Because of the habit of some bucks to approach around the back, as it were, one needs as near all-round visibility as possible from your calling place. It is better to stand up against a tree (to break

---

Hints for the Month

- Calling is daytime work – be extra careful about safety.
- Take your Firearm Certificate with you on all stalking outings. Don't put the bolt in the rifle until you are on your ground.
- Don't over-stalk one area, or over-call one buck. They soon get the idea.
- Take a face veil and insect repellent.

---

your silhouette) than to sit down, or to choose a valley, for example, where one can look across and into the bushes on the opposite slope. Remember that a buck is more likely to respond to the call within his own territory. Luring him out of cover is fifty times harder than meeting him on his own ground so pinpointing the bucks and their territories beforehand is vital, as is locating likely places giving reasonable visibility without being completely open. The sort of place which is good for calling (always provided that it lies in a territory or very nearby) is a stand of well-grown larch with a ground cover of brambles, a straggle of bushes with open spaces between, or a thicket of scrubby ash and maple such as one often finds on the steeper chalk slopes. In the conifer forests, the best chances are along any watercourses, frost pockets where the trees have failed and newly replanted areas where regrowth has started.

Can one call from a high seat? Lots of the experts say you can't, but my bucks do not seem to have read the right books. Maybe one could say that once a buck has come to a lure from a high seat *and has rumbled the stalker sitting up there*, he probably has sense enough not to do the same thing again, at least that season.

You will read very precise instructions about the number of peeps which one should make at a time, but if you are lucky enough to see a doe when she is squeaking and in search of a buck, she goes on most of the time! My Hungarian tutor squeaked for about a minute, waited a bit for something to happen and then did the same again. If that didn't work, he would swap calls and make the next session with the two-tone *pee-eh*. Where most people go wrong is impatience: if nothing appears after five minutes, they decide to move and the buck which may have been ambling in from a couple of hundred yards away finds his bird flown! Yes, sometimes they will come like a springer spaniel after a rabbit – but not often, and then it is usually a young hopeful, not the heavy old stager you hoped to outwit. One needs to visualise what may

If nothing comes immediately to your call, do not be in a hurry to move away. A buck may have heard but is cautious in his approach. He may circle downwind of you, so look out all round.

be going on behind the screen of leaves, and give the possible buck at the least ten minutes *by your watch* after the last set of calls. The way your senses and expectations are screwed up, there is no way of estimating time without that check. A minute seems like half an hour; ten an eternity. Standing really still is not encouraged in our everyday life.

What is the best time and weather? Every stalker has experience of calling succeeding under the most unlikely conditions. One can only lay down general guidelines. Too much wind makes the call difficult to hear. Cold, heavy rain is discouraging to both buck and caller. The classic calling weather is hot and heavy with a thundery feel to the air, but warm drizzle is not bad. The likeliest times are between 9.30 a.m. and 3.00 p.m. Maybe this is because the roe have been busy all night and need a period of rest before taking up the chase once more.

Another point about calling is not to be impatient. After moving to your chosen spot, let things quieten down before calling. You never know, a buck may have heard a suspicious noise and unless alarmed may come to investigate. Calling can continue for some minutes but afterwards do not give up in disgust and move off. Not every buck comes galloping to the tryst, although some do. That's when it gets exciting! Be extra careful about safety when calling, and not only because the shot offered may be a quick one. Calling is most successful during the day so the ever-present question of safety is, if possible, even more extreme. These days people

The traditional method of calling roe using a stretched beech leaf.

are likely to be about in the woods at all times of day or night, but there are more of them in daytime, plus those whose work takes them there. The cardinal rule that no shot should be taken without a solid earth background must never be relaxed in the sudden excitements of calling, nor should it be forgotten that deer are not the only creatures to respond to a call. Buzzards and foxes are frequently lured in – but so is the inquisitive passer-by, hearing a strange and interesting noise. So enjoy the breathless excitement of the roe rut – but be extra careful!

September

> **Hints for the Month**
>
> - Review your cull target. Have you shot enough yearling bucks? If not, now is the time.
> - Pace out the range after each shot and brush up on range estimation.
> - Look at any farm stock in the fields: are they wandering and feeding or lying under a hedge sheltering? The deer are likely to be doing the same.

'I've got all my mature bucks, but there's a few yearlings left to find.' Does that strike a familiar chord? The weather was bad in April and by the time the roe began to show up you were into May and serious trophy stalking. That is how the essential business of thinning out yearling bucks gets behind. Stalkers, especially guests, are often reluctant to polish off a yearling in case the shot spoils a chance at something better. From June onwards the new leaves and bracken turn many woods into a minor jungle. So September is a fine time to catch up with any deficit in the cull.

Stubble fields are often a draw to deer now that straw burning has come to an end. A good many roe and fallow spend a lot of time concealed in the growing corn where they are safe from stalkers and probably less bothered by flies. Harvest leaves them

In hill districts, roe tend to haunt the margin between wood and moorland.

completely exposed and disoriented so that the first days after a field is cleared can be a bonanza – specially if a scatter of big bales gives one a chance to sneak out (or lie out) in the middle. Later the spilt grain and other seeds start to germinate, offering very nutritious grazing when browse in the woods is getting rather stale. Yearlings which have been unseen in your own woods all summer will be out morning and evening where they may well be joined by some which emigrated at the time of the cast-out in May but which tend to drift back towards autumn. Numbers on the fields can be observed and counted. It's not too late to have a rethink about the total number of yearling bucks on the shooting plan. The number of does showing up can also be something of a surprise.

Tactics for field stalking are another ball-game compared to classic woodland stalking. A careful Highland-style long-distance spy is advisable. In fact where the countryside is very open a telescope can be instructive and may save a wasted stalk after something which in the end you don't want to shoot. The deer know they are exposed and use their eyes – and their legs – in response to distant movement. Their car-recognition is good, too. The farm Land Rover or tractor can come and go without attracting much notice, but try doing the same with your own vehicle and see the difference! Maybe it's not cheating to sit on the tail-board and get decanted behind a big bale, but even that won't work very often before the game is rumbled. If influence can be exerted to leave one or two bales in tactical places after the rest have been carted they can make extremely useful hides to get on terms with those maddening groups of deer which lie far out, laughing at efforts to

Big conifer blocks make difficult stalking unless the forest has been designed, as here, to leave wide rides and with any valley bottoms and watercourses unplanted. Occasional willows planted along the timber edge will attract roe where they can be seen. *(Photo L Guthrie)*

stalk them. A camouflage net laced with straw and laid flat with you underneath it is worth trying if you are willing to go out in the late afternoon and lie motionless, if necessary until dusk. Take a good book and a flask of tea!

Combine straw makes good cover for a flat crawl, but having got into range the critical thing is to think how to get enough elevation without revealing yourself to already suspicious deer. The only hope for a steady prone shot is to have a bipod ready fitted to the rifle. Probably you will need one of the longer types so that you can take a sitting shot. I prefer the sort which allows a certain amount of tilt without having to fiddle with the leg adjustments to get the weapon level and avoid missed shots due to cant. Playing with set screws and springs while those critical seconds tick away is bad for the soul. Shots may also be at rather longer range than has been necessary in the woods and range estimation from prone is exceptionally difficult.

For your own confidence a zeroing session is advisable. Depending on calibre, a group at 100 m which prints about 4 cm (1½ in) high will iron out most range misjudgements up to the point where the deer looks too small through the scope. Nor is absolute range the only criterion in deciding whether to take any particular shot. Slow breathing and a steady hold may be difficult to achieve after a long crawl and usually there are several knife-sharp stones pressing into tender parts of one's anatomy, all contributing to a shooting position which is far removed from the stress-free, comfortably sloped firing point at your local range. Before loosing off, take a critical look down the scope: is the reticle steady on target, or (be honest) are you hoping to catch it on the swing? If owners of vari-power scopes are tempted at this point to wind up the magnification, the deer is almost certainly too far off *for the conditions at that moment*. Too far may be over 200 m or less than 70. It may even now be possible to get a bit closer, or at least improve your firing position to get a steadier shot. Once that bullet has gone, you either have a wounded deer or an empty field. Do not risk it; take a little extra trouble.

Selecting which yearlings to shoot depends on two things: how much you like to play with theory, and how pressed you are to get numbers before the end of the season! The theory is that one cannot tell what antlers a buck will grow in later life from its yearling head. If you can distinguish which yearlings have had a good start in life from their body size and condition and which are stunted or thin, it stands to reason that one should select from the latter group. However, where living is plush, as it is over large parts of southern England and much of the east coast of Scotland, most of the young bucks will be in good order by now and it is much more important to cull out the right proportion of this age class than it is to agonise over which one should be spared and which shot. You will end the season still with 'a few yearlings to find', and that is poor deer management.

October

> **Hints for the Month**
>
> - Deer are very obvious on farm crops. Do you regularly contact farm staff about marauding? Now is a good time.
> - It's a nervous time for the gamekeeper – contact him too and collaborate to the full.
> - Review your doe cull target in view of what has been seen through the summer.
> - Check high seats for rot or rust. Re-site or remove portables ready for use in the doe season.

October is a month when you can slack off – if your buck cull is complete, your observations and plans for the doe season satisfactory and your high seats spruced-up and if necessary repositioned in preparation for the needs of the doe cull. In Scotland you can make a flying start on this from 21 October, which is not a bad idea in case of bad weather later in the winter.

'Be careful how you go up that seat on the cross rides,' says the returning stalker. 'The top rung is dodgy!' Does that warning strike a familiar bell? High seats have been with us for many years now and not to put it too crudely, a good many of them may have been safe once but with the lapse of time are now death-traps.

Even if you fall out of a seat yourself and break your silly neck, somebody is likely to be sorry, but if it's a visitor who does a backward somersault off the top of one of your seats it is unprofessional at best and at worst you may be liable for substantial damages and a conviction under the Health and Safety Regulations. Now is as good a time as any to make a point of going round your seats to check them thoroughly before the busy season. For example, a penknife can be used to test for decay on wooden seats – push it into the uprights just at ground level where rot is likely to start. Have the safety signs been removed? Jump on the centre of each rung (holding on as you do so), and bounce on the plank seat to simulate the restless weight of two men, one at least of whom might easily weigh twenty stone judging by some of my past guests! The thing is that while you tend to go up a rickety seat yourself with extra precaution standing on the ends of each rung, a visitor heaves his sometimes massive weight up by treading in the middle. If the distance between rungs is a bit much for him, he will put even more strain on them.

Sitting quietly with a client one evening, he remarked that there was a curious creaking noise from somewhere. Soon afterwards

the plank we occupied folded in two, depositing us on the floor of the seat. There was a large knot in it which had failed with the extra burden. Another elderly client stepped heavily on the top rung, broke it, and descended to the next, which also broke. Fortunately the demolition stopped at that point but it could have been nasty. He was quite good about it, but such mishaps should not happen.

These days, high seats have to conform to specifications laid down under the Health and Safety Regulations. For example wooden rungs must

A portable high seat is very useful for making a quick response to complaints of farm damage.

be notched into the uprights and wired in place, not only up the poles, but across each rung so that the accident I have described should not happen. Rails must be fitted to prevent anyone falling out. Responsibility for design and maintenance lies firmly with the Occupier. If you pay for your stalking this may be you! (To avoid serious problems under the modern stalker's statutory obligations you should study Appendix 6 very carefully.) One liability which can seem a bit unreasonable concerns the passer-by, trespasser or not, who may be tempted to scale a high seat to his injury. In these days when people are quick to sue – especially if they don't like the idea of shooting Bambis anyway – any high seat which is past its sell-by date should be pulled down. So, too, with any that have out-lived their use, for example when a plantation grows up and blocks the view. Take them away or break them up, but don't leave unnecessary temptations about to create trouble.

Metal seats also need maintenance. Even the ones which don't come to bits need painting and those which do have a nasty habit of rusting up the spigot joints without constant greasing. Steel tubes rust internally even if the outside is kept painted, and this insidious damage is hard to detect. If the tube has no drain holes, water seeping in freezes and bursts it, usually at the most critical place near ground level.

When I first started making seats, they were made without conscious thought to suit my rather lanky build. This led to complaints from visitors that sitting on a plank so high that their feet could not touch the floor became extremely painful after an hour or so. Added to that, if a buck did emerge they were unable to aim the rifle because the slits were too high! After a time, one learns. A comfortable shooting position makes for accuracy even among the buck-fevered.

Of course, the lean-to sort has to use a solid support, otherwise in any sort of wind the tree's movement is enough to make straight shooting almost impossible. If a lissom tree just has to be used it's best to cut the top off just above the seat – but not before asking the Forester!

November

Doe shooting is something which has to be done, whether we like the idea or not. Anyone with a grain of common sense can see that the increase of any animal population can only be limited by controlling the number of breeding females and limiting deer numbers is a very high priority in the minds of most stalkers these days. If stalking is regarded purely as fun, which was indeed the case until after the Second World War then there is no doubt that strolling the summer woods in search of a big six-pointer buck is the cream of it. As late as 1951, Henry Tegner, one of the founding fathers of roe stalking wrote in his book *The Sporting Rifle in Britain* *'Normally one does not go after a roe doe with the rifle. The roe stalker regards the female as the potential mother of a fine head.'* Very soon afterwards he was open-minded enough to modernise his ideas and became an enthusiastic advocate of adequate doe culling.

Hints for the Month

- Plan to take **at least** as many does as your buck cull, more if you want to reduce numbers.
- Do not attempt to select old or sick does, but take them when the chance comes.
- Don't delay the doe cull until late winter. Start now if you can.
- Remember that all roe does, but not bucks, have a downward-pointing tuft of hair in the tail patch. Bucks are shedding their antlers and may be difficult to identify unless you check.
- Be extra safety-conscious: many people are about the countryside during doe-stalking hours.
- Do not be tempted to take long or fancy shots. Roe in winter coat only seem to look bigger.

Having watched those charming little family groups all summer, it takes an effort of will to take the rifle to them from November onwards, but the job has to be done and unless you only have one or two to shoot, it is no good putting it off until January or February. By that time the weather will be bad and the days short. All too soon it's the end of the season and you haven't done enough to serve the interests of your landlord – or indeed of the deer themselves.

The farmland stalker will find there will still be good feeding for deer in the fields and along the hedgerows. Autumn-sown crops will also attract parties of deer. In south-country woods there should be plenty of bramble and ivy leaves and enough cover to keep the deer in much the same places as they have been all summer. They will be easier to spot, but of course so will the stalker! Even greater care and stealth is needed. The crisp fallen leaves or crusted snow can sometimes make one feel one is trudging through a six-inch layer of cornflakes. Watch out when woodpigeon numbers build up. Deer will certainly take note of their flapping panic flight and can track your progress through

Look before you shoot! The kid on the left is a buck. The doe kid is on the right – note the distinguishing anal tush. *(Photo Robin Lowes)*

the wood by this means even if the wind and everything else are in your favour. I know one or two coverts where it is better to start stalking later in the morning when the grey hordes have flown off to breakfast. In any case there tends to be more deer movement during the short winter days than one could expect in summer.

Over much of the country this is a worrying time for the gamekeeper, and every stalker must lean over backwards to understand any reservations which he may have about your wandering about early and late when he is trying so hard to keep his birds safe and present them well on shooting days. Maintain good contact with him and go along with any reasonable restrictions he may impose. Besides anything, there is more money involved in game shooting than stalking. After a season or two things may relax as he sees that you grasp his problems and are prepared to go along with them. Another man on the ground at unscheduled hours has advantages for the keeper, too. If you keep away from the release pens in the evening to avoid putting birds off roost and leave things quiet on the day of a shoot and the one before, stalking need not disrupt the smooth running of a shoot.

Unless you have very few to shoot, don't attempt to select the does you shoot. Virtually all female deer, including this season's kids, will be breeding next year and for sure if you try to be too particular your total will be short of the planned cull come 1 March. In the north, where snow and other severe weather can be expected, there is a good argument early in the season for weeding out the second kid from a pair of twins, leaving the mother with just one which will benefit from her lead and example at least until later in the winter. If it comes to the crunch, however, it is numbers which count and if there are too many deer on the ground they themselves will suffer. The refinements come a long way after this imperative.

Ranges tend to be longer in winter, so it pays to check the zero on your rifle. There will be likely to be more chances of a prone

Even when under pressure to get does do not relax the rules of safety. This would be a dangerous shot.

shot after the cover is off, and a bipod may be invaluable. If you use one, fit it on before zeroing because it may change the point of impact – and that is something you really need to know!

The other difference between the buck and doe seasons is that although the deer look bigger because of their fluffy coats, the doe is usually smaller and her neck in particular makes a very slim target indeed. If you are very close, a shot at the base of the neck can safely be taken, but farther up the vital area is small, and of course highly mobile. So do not be tempted to take fancy shots in an effort to save a bit of damage to the shoulder – you may lose the lot! A solid broadside shot in the boiler-house – *after* you have checked that revealing backside tuft – is far the best.

December

Hints for the Month

- If your ground is a pheasant shoot, offer to do a day's beating. You may see odd corners which you never visit when stalking.
- Don't be a dog in the manger – if you have a lot of does to get, share with somebody who hasn't got much stalking.
- Have a good first aid kit in the car: knives and cold hands can make for nasty cuts.
- Keep your tetanus jabs up to date.

As their natural food gets shorter, especially in the north, roe may start feeding seriously on àny root crops grown for the sheep.

To stop deer raiding a field effectively is never easy, and because of safety, the actual shooting may be difficult, with many opportunities for a shot having to be passed up. On the other hand, complaints of deer raiding the fields have so many times been the entrée for a would-be stalker. Seize the chance to demonstrate that you can be relied on to do a conscientious job for the farmer, neither greedy for venison or trophies or unreliable no matter what the weather throws at you, when you have promised to defend a certain crop. That is often the start – or the end – of a promising stalking career!

A portable high seat can be extremely useful in places where shots at ground level may be dangerous. If soon after he has phoned you a farmer sees a high seat put up overlooking the vulnerable field he will feel that the stalker is on his side. The sound of a bang the next morning, and maybe the offer of a fresh roe liver and your reputation is made in the district! Success often depends on good reconnaissance: walk round the field looking for points where the deer have entered; identify places where a safe shot would be possible, taking note of farm buildings and footpaths and ask about where any farm animals are likely to be for the next few days. If any doubt put up that high seat and make sure that the arcs of fire are free of branches. Plan approach routes so that you can get to your selected firing point unseen, bearing in mind the direction of the wind.

One sharp lesson may be enough to keep the deer away until the crop is eaten off, but leave your phone number so that they will let you know if the problem continues without your having to waste time on an unnecessary visit.

The Christmas holidays offer the best time to introduce a beginner to woodland stalking – not least to make him realise that there is more to it than swanning out on a fine summer morning to try for a roe buck! Visibility is good, and although it tends to be a difficult period in the doe season a beginner is saved those agonising decisions about whether a beast ought to be shot or spared which mark the buck season. Under the conditions we enjoy in this country, with a super-abundant deer population heavily biased towards the doe, the decisions facing a stalker are limited to choosing a beast which is definitely female, clear of its fellows and a safe, sure shot to take.

Any aspiring stalker who is lucky enough to have connections in the country or who knows a professional who is big-hearted enough to be prepared to take time and trouble over a tyro may have the chance to learn the old-fashioned way in the company of an experienced guide. Make no mistake – you are asking a very considerable favour of such a man and he will know that his own

How many does have twins? This is your first indication of breeding success, and so of the proper cull.

chances to complete his cull will be seriously prejudiced just by your presence, let alone by your bungling efforts.

Lacking that opening, or to make much better use of it when it comes, you can go on a beginner's stalking course. At least you will be taught the basics on which to build your technique. Such courses vary in length and content but those run by the B.D.S. and B.A.S.C. represent excellent value for money. They cover species identification and natural history, law, safety, stalking technique and marksmanship. Usually there will be a session on the range, giving everyone the chance to fire with their own or a borrowed rifle and to understand about trajectory and zeroing. Courses based on the excellent Deer Stalking Certificate syllabus finish with a test, successful candidates being issued with a Level One certificate. That does not imply that you are a finished stalker, only that you have taken in the basics of the subject. It is the springboard to higher things! More information about stalking courses can be found in Appendix 5.

January

Pressure on most stalkers builds up at this time of year to get on with the doe cull. Pheasant shooting continues but the keeper is less pressed, so access to some coverts is easier. The deer tend to feed in the fields, which gives new opportunities and new challenges, but it can take a bit of resolution to face the weather! Deer need to be visible, feeding, loafing in the sun or whatever, otherwise you probably won't see them. What you have to do

If you are lucky you may find a cast antler. Older bucks tend to cast first, younger animals up to Christmas.

is anticipate what they are *likely* to be doing – and then go and see if they really are. In bad weather they may be doing nothing!

While a gentle warm rain hurts nobody, deer dislike being cold and wet. A sudden storm may possibly provoke a bit of movement as they seek a more comfortable, sheltered spot. Sunshine after   rain brings them out, and it is worth enduring some discomfort to be in the right spot as the clouds roll away and the deer stand up, shake themselves, get into a sunny spot and nibble one of the Forester's trees, just to express their general wellbeing. Continuous cold rain, especially when driven by a sharp wind, drives them into the deepest cover, into the lee of hedges and anywhere else where it is difficult to find them.

Heavy snowfall has a disorientating effect which is quite understandable as the whole aspect of the habitat must be altered. There may be a short period of frantic feeding before a storm if the animals sense its arrival, followed by a search for sheltered corners in which to lie up. I have noticed with roe that their activity is very much reduced in snow, which of course limits their need for food. In deep snow they make forms in it like hares, which must give good shelter. A depth of 30 cm (1 ft) seriously interferes with their mobility as they break through any light crust and have to progress in bounds.

Hints for the Month

- Take enough clothes to keep warm and dry. Take a layer off if you get hot, but replace it before you get chilled.
- Take spare dry gloves in the roe sack.
- A flask of hot coffee is better than alcohol.
- When everything is snow-covered, look for clear places under the trees.
- Fallen ivy-covered trees are a great draw to the roe.
- A gentle move to two or three experienced rifles can help to complete the cull.

Crusted snow makes stalking a nightmare. In snowy districts try to break the back of your doe cull early in the season.

When the ground is snow-covered it is worth looking for wind-swept places where feeding is still possible, or beneath heavy canopy conifers, particularly Douglas fir, where the ground may still be bare. The weight of snow often brings down a good harvest of green needles for the deer to enjoy.

From the stalker's own point of view, being cold, wet and generally miserable is not what it is all about. Besides anything else, rain on binoculars and scope, cold hands and so on not only take away from one's general enjoyment, but may so easily contribute to poor shooting. This is one of the essential differences between woodland and hill stalking. On the open hill both deer and man expect to be wet and miserable, it is an arduous and demanding sport. A regular woodland stalker has to weigh up the value of his going out under such conditions against the undoubted fact that he will be disturbing his deer, making them even shyer for next time and, in snow, using up their reserves of energy. If it is his only chance for a week or two, he just has to endure it, think where the deer may be lying and look for them there with the greatest care.

Wind alone has a very important influence on deer behaviour. Their world of scent, which we disregard at our peril, is carried on the air currents. A very dry wind makes deer nervous because it is a poor carrier of scent. In contrast, how often has one seen normally skittish deer as placid as cows on a warm, damp, misty morning.

As an addition to the does collected by stalking, certainly not as

Even if you know the beast is dead, each one you shoot on snow-covered ground leaves easy-to-follow traces which are educational to follow for stalker and dog.

an alternative, it may be possible to organise a gentle move (see page 107). Some places lend themselves to minor manoeuvres done by two collaborators: small copses connected by hedges or well-used deer tracks which can be ambushed by one while the other quietly stalks the copse itself. Stream-side withy bushes and alder carrs or hanging woods on steep slopes often lend themselves to this sort of scheme. The main thing is that the cover is in no way 'beaten', but disturbed as gently as possible, so that the rifle in ambush is presented with deer which are walking slowly, often looking back at the danger they are avoiding. He must have time to identify the sex of whatever comes, and take a leisured shot at a stationary target. These schemes can go on during the middle of the day and should not take the place of traditional stalking or high-sitting at dusk and dawn. They can produce a welcome bonus of does – or be totally disastrous. If it works once – do not try it again until next winter!

Anything larger-scale than this, involving several rifles and bigger stretches of woodland, needs the most careful planning, inspired placing of high seats and considerable self-control on the part of the rifles. Everyone goes as quietly as possible to their seats to wait events. This movement in itself is enough to put the deer on foot, and the first shot tends to move them towards another seat where the same reception awaits them. The whole operation

Shooting does on farm crops may scare the rest away. If the roots are useful as a magnet, it is better not to shoot on the field itself, but on the approaches. *(Photo Jeppe)*

should be done with the least disturbance. One or more walkers may or may not be necessary in very large forests. Experience and good feedback from participants refine the plans for next year!

It is best to choose a mild, calm day. Windy or frosty weather tends to make deer nervous and inclined to move fast and far. Roe tend to run when disturbed, but trickle back to their accustomed haunts. This tendency was made use of by Ronnie Rose, that old Master of the Borders. His scheme was to move the deer out of a block of forestry *before* stationing his rifles. They would then be posted facing away from the block just moved, to shoot the roe as they came slowly back.

In any of these efforts to supplement the doe cull the whole idea is to move the deer without alarming them, and to ambush them in places where they tend to hesitate, giving the rifle every chance for a deliberate shot. The large-scale deer drives which disgraced our country until comparatively recently produced a horrifying number of crippled or mortally wounded animals and a substantial risk to the participants. Nothing remotely resembling them must ever be allowed to return, no matter what pressures there may be to limit deer numbers. It is up to us as legitimate stalkers to avoid that situation by getting on with a full cull, and doing it humanely.

February

> **Hints for the Month**
>
> - If you aren't seeing many does but are still short of your target, don't reduce it. They will all show up again when the open season is over!
> - Last year's kids count equally with mature does – they would be breeding this coming year.
> - Take note of the number of surviving kids per doe. This is basic information in planning next season's shooting targets.

Many stalkers who are trying to do a conscientious job with a heavy doe cull feel an increasing distaste for shooting ever more obviously pregnant females. A Danish friend was talking the other day about the next visit to his stalking ground in the south of England. 'I'll enjoy having a look round when I come in February, see how the roe have wintered, and maybe I'll try to find a yearling doe to shoot.'

It is a nice bit of ground with hazel copses and biggish fields – ideal habitat for roe. It happened that a few days before I had had an earful from one of the tenant farmers about the number of deer about, so I suggested that it might be a good idea to be a bit more aggressive, not only in defence of the crops but in his own interests, if he wanted to have some decent heads to stalk next summer. 'Oh! I don't really like killing does at that time of year – they are all pregnant and you are really killing three!'

You can imagine the discussion which developed. Good bucks, I said, like peace and quiet – not too many does competing for browse and complaining about bringing muddy hooves into the territory, or whatever it is bothers male roe. Not only that, but any doe that finds herself unaccompanied by a buck next July will go out and drag the nearest surplus yearling back to her own home range, thus nullifying all the stalker's efforts to reduce this age-class on his patch. Somehow, I didn't feel that there was much of a meeting of minds, even though it was refreshing to meet somebody who was really keen about his roe but who wasn't judging his pleasure by the number of slain.

Most stalkers have more than a twinge when faced with their duty to get on with the doe cull, even though most do realise that reducing the numbers of breeding females is a fundamental necessity for good management under conditions which apply over most of the country. In our part of the world the mild climate and abundant feeding mean not only that the conception rate is high, but a high proportion of the kids survive into the next spring. For the same reasons, once a kid reaches the age of five months it is unlikely to suffer by being orphaned. In areas where heavy and prolonged snowfall is a normal part of the winter, matters may be different because the adults forge paths through the drifts and their young are able to follow.

The build-up of high population densities due to under-culling will be limited to some extent by emigration, provided there is anywhere for the yearlings to go when they are pushed out in spring. However, roe will not self-regulate to a population level which is satisfactory for their own health, let alone the peace of mind of the foresters and farmers at whose expense they exist. The more breeding does, the more yearlings next year and the more curry-hot telephone calls from discontented landlords. Too many of those, and you have lost your stalking!

Coming back to my Danish friend, other countries have their own problems to face and their own solutions to work out, often with a background of a much greater shooting pressure than in Britain, which means much smaller doe culls to be achieved by each individual stalker. Some visitors who stalk over here quickly recognise this and adapt their attitude. Others find the mental leap rather indigestible. To them, our own somewhat ruthless approach to the doe cull may appear totally lacking in respect for a noble quarry, and maybe we are not too good at demonstrating to our visitors either the abundance of the population or the care and affection which we do actually give them. If a visitor gets his own patch to stalk without supervision it is understandable if he applies the rules which he learned at home. If he is lucky, a hard-working stalker next door has to take care of the outgoing surplus yearlings, otherwise he may express surprise after two or three years that the quality of his trophies doesn't seem as good as it was to begin with. He may invent all sorts of reasons for this, from poaching to disease or **over**-shooting, but the truth, as ever, is likely to be hard to take on board.

Deer warbles occasionally affect Scottish roe. They are not the same as cattle warbles. As they lie under the skin, the meat need not be condemned.

Colour variation. Black roe are rare but are seen from time to time. *(Photo M Howell)*

The argument about 'killing three' by shooting a doe in February is not, of course a valid one, as all breeding does are pregnant throughout the open season. It is one's own distaste which grows with the foetus. I remember my embarrassment when my landlord's wife, who had just had a baby, asked me if the doe I had shot that evening had been pregnant. I had to say yes, to which she replied, 'Well, if I had to be shot I'd prefer that it was done before I had to go through actually having the baby!' Something from the horse's mouth, as you might say.

A good deal of ink is spilled over selecting does for culling, choosing only the old or those with poor kids and so on. Maybe if one had the whole of the season to shoot just two or three does from a modest patch of woodland then one might be able to pick out certain individuals at leisure without under-shooting to the ultimate detriment of the deer. I would think that the majority of readers who take their stalking at all seriously, whether as paying guests or lessees of stalking, have as many or more does to account for than they have time to spend. It is best to take a random slice of the population from old does to last summer's kids. Do not invariably select the biggest! When the pressure is on, the 'Rule of Three' applies:

1. Is it female?
2. Is it safe?
3. Am I confident enough to take the shot?

The older bucks will already be forward in velvet by the end of February. Make a note of them! *(Photo J Poutsma)*

Think of the old-fashioned schoolmaster walloping away at some unfortunate pupil, saying as he does so 'I am only doing this for your own good!' Maybe he had something – or not – but it certainly applies to a resolute approach to the doe cull.

Very soon now the year will have turned and we can all think with renewed excitement of the delights of summer buck stalking, perhaps even with more pleasure at the thought of an honest job of the doe cull satisfactorily completed.

Main Legislation Affecting Deer

The information in this book is based on legislation applying on 1 January 1999. Stalkers should attempt to keep themselves up to date on changes. In case of doubt apply to the B.D.S., Game Conservancy or B.A.S.C. for assistance.

The principal legislation which applies to deer is as follows:

Deer

England and Wales
The Game Licences Act 1860
Deer Act 1991 (D A 91)
Deer Act 1980
Wildlife & Countryside Act 1981

Scotland
Sale of Venison (Scotland) Act 1968
Deer (Firearms etc.) (Scotland) Order 1985 No. 1168
Deer (Scotland) Act 1996 (D A (S) 96)

Firearms

Firearms Act 1968
Firearms (Amendment) Acts 1988, 1992, 1997
Firearms Rules 1998

Northern Ireland
The Wildlife (Northern Ireland) Order 1985

The sale of venison

England and Wales
Venison may only be sold to a licensed game dealer (D A 91, section 10). Venison may not be purchased by a licensed game dealer during the prohibited period except from another licensed game or venison dealer. (The prohibited period for any species and description of deer for which a close season is prescribed means the period beginning with the expiry of the tenth day and ending with the expiry of the last day of that season.)

Buying, selling or receiving venison taken illegally is an offence (D A 91, section 10).

Licensed game dealers must keep records which may be inspected by an authorised officer or constable who may also inspect any venison in the dealer's possession (D A 91, section 11).

'Sale' and 'purchase' include barter and exchange.

'Venison' includes imported venison and means any edible part of the carcass of a deer which has not been cooked or canned.

Scotland

Venison may only be sold to or purchased from a licensed venison dealer (D A (S) 96, section 36). Licensed venison dealers must keep records which may be inspected by persons authorised by the Secretary of State or Deer Commission for Scotland, or any constable, who may also inspect any venison in a dealer's possession. Buying, selling, or receiving venison taken illegally is an offence.

'Sale' and 'purchase' includes barter and exchange.

'Venison' includes the carcass or any edible part of a deer.

Statutory close seasons

Species	Sex	England & Wales	Scotland	Northern Ireland
Red	Stags	1 May – 31 July	21 October – 30 June	1 May – 31 July
	Hinds	1 March – 31 October	16 February – 20 October	1 March – 31 October
Red/Sika Hybrids	Stags		21 October – 30 June	
	Hinds		16 February – 20 October	
Sika	Stags	1 May – 31 July	21 October – 30 June	1 May – 31 July
	Hinds	1 March – 31 October	16 February – 20 October	1 March – 31 October
Fallow	Bucks	1 May – 31 July	1 May – 31 July	1 May – 31 July
	Does	1 March – 31 October	16 February – 20 October	1 March – 31 October
Roe	Bucks	1 November – 31 March	21 October – 31 March	
	Does	1 March – 31 October	1 April – 20 October	

Muntjac and Chinese water deer: no legal close season. They are, however, covered by the legislation regarding the use of rifles for killing deer.

Ballistics of Popular Cartridges

Calibre Bullet weight	Velocity – Feet per sec Muzzle 100 yd 200 yd			Energy – foot pounds Muzzle 100 yd 200 yd			Sight at yd	+ = point of impact above – = point of impact below				
								25	50	100	150	200
.222 Rem 50 gr/3.2 g	3200	2650	2170	1137	780	520	100	−0.8	−0.3	0	−0.9	−3.2
.223 Rem 55gr/3.5g	3240	2747	2304	1282	921	648	100	−0.8	−0.4	0	−1.0	−3.8
.22-250 53gr/3.4g	3707	3192	2741	1616	1198	883	100	−0.9	−0.4	0	−0.5	−1.9
.243 Win 100gr/6.5g	3070	2790	2540	2090	1730	1430	100	−0.7	−0.2	0	−0.9	−2.9
.270 Win 130gr/8.4g	3140	2884	2639	2847	2401	2011	100	−0.8	−0.3	0	−0.8	−2.7
.270 Win 150gr/9.7g	2800	2616	2436	2616	2280	1977	100	−0.7	−0.2	0	−1.1	−3.6
6.5 x 55 139gr/9.0g	2854	2691	2533	2512	2233	1978	100	−0.7	−0.2	0	−1.0	−2.3
.275 Rigby 140gr/9.0g	2750	2325	1960	2575	1867	1326	100	−0.7	−0.1	0	−1.0	−3.5
7mmx57 150gr/9.7g	2755	2539	2331	2530	2148	1810	100	−0.7	−0.1	0	−1.2	−3.9
7mm Rem Mag 150gr/9.7g	3250	2960	2690	3519	2919	2410	100	−0.8	−0.3	0	−0.7	−2.4
7mmx64 150gr/9.7g	2890	2625	2375	2779	2295	1879	100	−0.7	−0.2	0	−1.0	−3.3
30-06 130gr/8.4g	3205	2876	2561	2966	2388	1894	100	−0.8	−0.3	0	−0.8	−2.7
30-06 150gr/9.7g	2970	2680	2402	2943	2393	1922	100	−0.7	−0.2	0	−1.0	−3.4
.308 Win 130gr/8.4g	2900	2590	2300	2428	1937	1527	100	−0.7	−0.2	0	−1.1	−3.7
308 Win 150gr/9.7g	2860	2570	2300	2725	2200	1760	100	−0.7	−0.2	0	−1.2	−3.8
.308 Win 180gr/11.6g	2610	2400	2210	2725	2303	1952	100	−0.6	−0.1	0	−1.4	−4.5

Reproduced from Parker-Hale, Norma and Rigby ballistic data.

Reading List

Recent publications

Alcock, I. *Chasing the Red Deer and Following the Roe* (Sauchenyard Press) 1998

Carne, P. *Woodland Stalking* (Swan Hill Press) 1999

Danilkin, A. *Behavioural Ecology of Siberian and European Roe Deer* (Chapman & Hall) 1996

Prior, R. *The Roe Deer – Conservation of a Native Species* (Swan Hill Press) 1995

Prior, R. *Trees and Deer* (Swan Hill Press) 1994

Prior, R. *Deer Management in Small Woodlands* (Game Conservancy) 1987

Putman, R. *The Natural History of Deer* (Helm) 1988

Further reading

If you want to dig into the literature of roe, send for lists from specialist booksellers such as David Grayling (Verdun House, Shap, Penrith, Cumbria CA10 3JP), Paul Morgan (Coch-y-Bonddu Books, Papyrus, Pentrehedyn Street, Machynlleth, Wales SY20 8DJ); John and Judith Head (The Barn Book Supply, 88 Crane Street, Salisbury, SP1 2QD, Wilts).

Here are a few titles to look out for:-

Chaplin, R. *Capreolus* (Collins) 1978

Holmes, F. *Following the Roe* (Bartholomew) 1974

Page, F. J. T. *Field Guide to British Deer* (Blackwell) 1982

Prior, R. *Roe Deer of Cranborne Chase* (Oxford) 1968

Prior, R. *Modern Roe Stalking* (Tideline) 1985

'Snaffle' *The Roe Deer* (Harwar) 1904 (Reprinted Ashford Press) 1987

Tegner, H. *The Buck of Lordenshaw* (Batchworth) 1953

Tegner H. *The Roe Deer* (Reprinted Tideline) 1981

Whitehead, G. K. *Practical Deer Stalking* (Constable) 1986

Whitehead, G. K. *The Deer of Great Britain and Ireland* (Routledge & Kegan Paul) 1964

Williamson, R. *Capreol* (Macdonald) 1973

Other books by G. K. Whitehead, Frank Wallace, J. G. Millais and Henry Tegner contain much useful information on roe.

APPENDIX 4

C.I.C. Trophy Measuring

U.K. Trophy Commission members offering an official trophy measuring service:

Dominic Griffith, Penwood Grange, Penwood, Newbury, Berks, RG15 9EW

Allan Allison, The Bungalow, East Brackley, Kinross, KY13 7LU

Richard Prior, Chase Walk, Gussage All Saints, Wimborne, Dorset, BH21 5ET

Iain Watson, Mac Cottage, Sawne Road, Oakley, Kinross, KY12 9LA

Organisations Providing
Training and Advice on Deer

The British Deer Society (B.D.S.)

The Society was established in 1962. Many of the founders of the British Deer Society were closely involved in pressing for legislation to protect deer. Modern laws in the form of the Deer Acts to regulate the conservation, management, seasons and methods of culling deer were introduced into Scotland in 1959 and in England and Wales in 1963, mainly as a result of their efforts. These Acts have since been considerably amended.

At a national level, the Society organises symposia, training days and courses. New members usually become associated with the branch in whose area they reside, though they may opt for a different branch which, for a variety of reasons may be more convenient to them. Branch activities may include field meetings, lectures, educational visits to schools, shooting competitions and training, help with research projects, and putting on displays with an educational element at events such as country fairs, in addition to demonstrating what the Society is about and recruiting new members.

The majority of the foremost authorities on deer matters are members of the British Deer Society. It is therefore well placed to advise on any matter relating to deer. Much recent legislation emanating from Europe recently is likely to affect the welfare of British deer; such as Game Meat Hygiene, Firearms Licensing, Animal Welfare and Habitat Protection. In translating European Directives into British Law the Society's advice is frequently sought, and heeded, by government departments and other bodies with wide influence over matters concerning the treatment of deer.

Society training ranges from courses arranged in conjunction with formal training institutions, such as agricultural colleges, to courses arranged locally by B.D.S. branches. Deer stalkers form a large section of the Society's membership and their education about deer and the training, particularly of novice stalkers, in carrying out their role in a proper and humane manner is an important part of its activities. Certificates of achievement are offered and higher-level training leading to formal educational qualifications is being developed with colleges such as the Royal Agricultural College at Cirencester.

The Society's education programme aims to spread the knowledge of deer to all age and ability levels. A range of publications are available, from colouring books for the very young to study and resource packs for the student, teacher and youth leader. The B.D.S. Study and Resource Centre at Trentham in Staffordshire provides facilities for independent students or group visits. The centre also produces relevant display material and leaflets for both branch and National exhibitions.

Each year grants are also given to support important deer research, usually in conjunction with other concerned organisations. Practical help in the field is given to researchers by B.D.S. members and branches.

The Society's journal *Deer* is widely acclaimed and is sent to members four times a year. A junior news and project sheet *Oh Deer*, accompanies the journal to provide reading material for the family.

Contact: The British Deer Society, Burgate Manor, Fordingbridge, Hants SP6 1EF. Tel. 01425 655434; fax 01425 655433.

The British Association for Shooting and Conservation (B.A.S.C.)

B.A.S.C. is Britain's largest country shooting organisation. Supported by over 125,000 members, it represents and safeguards the interests of all those who enjoy shooting sports.

General shooting help and advice

- professional training for outside agencies on firearms use and conservation management
- assistance with certificate application, variation and renewal
- advice on police licensing departments and procedures
- general legal advice on firearms
- information on cartridge reloading
- advice on the suitability of firearms for particular types of quarry
- assistance with legal representation and access to expert witnesses for court cases relating to firearms
- cover for up to £5 million public liability insurance for all members, except supporters.

It is a representative body for both professional and recreational stalkers and deer managers, and is contributing to the formulation of government policy ensuring that all decision makers are aware that the most effective and humane method of managing deer is culling by shooting. B.A.S.C. is taking a leading role in setting the standards and providing training for both professional and recreational deer stalkers and deer managers.

B.A.S.C. provides:

- advice on all aspects of legislation, and theoretical and practical deer management
- advice on, and access to, accompanied stalking opportunities
- advice on deer management qualifications
- deer management courses leading to the Deer Stalking Certificate Levels One and Two.

It currently operates two stalking schemes in conjunction with the

Forestry Commission, primarily as a follow-on to stalking courses. The forests involved in this scheme are Kings Forest on the Norfolk/Suffolk border and Kershope Forest in Cumbria. It also operates a stalking scheme in conjunction with North West Water for the Deer Stalking Certificate Level Two training and assessment.

Contacts – Peter Watson or Emma George of the Deer Department. Direct dial telephone 01244 573025; fax: 01244 573 013; e-mail: peterw@basc.demon.co.uk

The Forestry Commission (F.C.)

F.C. runs a deer course aimed at deer managers. It is a management rather than a stalking course, and the target audience is rangers, stalkers, foresters, estate managers and landowners. The emphasis is on upland deer management and covers the management of red, roe and Sika deer. It is run at Torlundy Deer Training Centre, near Fort William.
Apply for details to the Forestry Commission, Lochaber Forest District, Torlundy, Fort William, Inverness-shire PH33 6SW. Tel. 01397 702184.

The Game Conservancy

The Advisory Service of Game Conservancy Limited has advised estates and farms on all aspects of game, their habitats and the species which share these habitats for over sixty years.
As the population of roe deer grows and spreads, growers, shoot owners and stalkers will increasingly come into contact with them. Advice is essential for all landowners who value their trees, new hedges and crops, and especially on the pheasant shoot to protect woodland planting and game crops. The correct management of roe deer as a sporting asset can also offset these costs.
Game Conservancy Limited runs management courses, many of which include sections on deer management. The Advisory Service can offer advice on any aspect of deer management from planning a cull and letting the stalking to minimising and controlling damage.
Apply for details to – Game Conservancy Limited, Advisory Service, Fordingbridge, Hants. SP6 1EF. Tel. 01425 652381.

Deer stalking qualifications

Deer stalking qualifications are administered by Deer Management Qualifications Ltd, Marford Mill, Rossett, Wrexham, Clwyd LL12 0HL.

Professional deer managers

In order to promote the highest standards among deer managers, **The U.K. Association of Professional Deer Managers** was set up in 1998. Membership is by election only. The aims of the Association are to

- enhance the standard and maintain the integrity of the deer stalking profession
- gain and maintain the confidence of landowners and their agents
- gain and maintain the confidence of client stalkers.

The Honorary Secretary is Christopher Borthen, Mill House, Thorverton, Devon EX5 5LX.

APPENDIX 6

Health, Safety and Hygiene Regulations Affecting the Stalker

By John Clifton-Bligh

Common and statute law both have a great deal to say about health and safety. These laws, as they apply to deer stalking, can be rather complicated, so when in doubt a wise stalker will turn to a properly qualified and competent lawyer for advice. These notes are not a substitute for that advice. They are intended only as a general guide to the health and safety aspects of recreational deer stalking. They do not cover the additional health and safety requirements that apply to stalkers who are employees, contractors or subcontractors.

Deer stalking activities with health and safety implications can conveniently be divided into two phases:

- everything leading up to and including the shooting of a deer
- everything involved in disposing of the dead animal

In the first phase, a person who is simply stalking with permission is a **visitor** to his ground. The owner or occupier's liability to visitors is restricted to the purposes for which they are permitted to enter the property and the owner or occupier is under no obligation for risks that his visiting stalker has willingly undertaken. Nevertheless, the owner or occupier has a common **duty of care** as well as a number of specific duties. He must ensure that:

- everyone directly involved with his land is aware of who is responsible for what
- the visiting stalker is informed and instructed on all the risks associated with his stalking ground, e.g. hazards, boundaries, rights of way and other users of the land (including the general public and trespassers)
- the stalker is able to enter and leave his ground safely
- the stalker is **qualified and competent** in all the activities his stalking may involve (the possession of certificates of qualification does not necessarily indicate competence, it is just one test of competence; other tests are the stalker's maturity and the extent and currency of his experience)
- all other users of the land, including the general public and trespassers are warned of the likely dangers of the stalker's activities; if necessary by displaying signs which comply with appropriate regulations

Having satisfied himself concerning the stalker's competence, the owner or occupier has a general duty to visit, review, revise and demand compliance with the instructions he has given.

For his part, the visiting stalker has a common duty of care to everyone who is affected by his activities. A stalker who has paid for the deer rights on his ground may have become the occupier of those rights. In that case, he will have assumed the occupier's health and safety responsibilities in relation to:

- everyone else who is directly involved with the land
- any visitor he is permitted to bring onto it
- the general public and trespassers

In discharging his responsibilities to all of these people, he must satisfy different requirements to provide sufficient information and instruction to each of three age groups:

- adults
- young persons (16–18 years old)
- children (less than 16 years old)

Any briefings he gives should be from written notes which include questions to confirm that the listener has understood the briefing. The notes he uses should be retained and updated at regular intervals.

An essential step in discharging all these responsibilities is the proper assessment of all the risks associated with the stalker's activities. Some guidance on **risk assessment** is given on page 184. The purpose is to keep all hazards **as low as reasonably practicable**.

The process of disposing of the dead animal must next be considered. The hazards of handling knives, lifting heavy carcasses, handling infected material and disposing of offal all require risk assessment. From the shot onwards, however, **food safety** is one of the most important areas of concern. This is because the dead animal will normally be converted into meat for human consumption. Whether the stalker sells, gives or otherwise disposes of the carcass, he is responsible for an important link in the food chain and he will be held to account for this responsibility. Some guidance on discharging it is given on page 186 under **Stalkers and Food Safety**.

Finally, a list of statutory instruments and codes of practice covering various aspects of deer stalking is included. The list is not necessarily exhaustive and stalkers should carefully check for other instruments that apply to their particular circumstances. Their risk assessments will help to point them in the right direction.

To summarise, the health and safety aspects of recreational deer stalking are governed by the law. Its foundation is the common **duty of care**. In a leading case this has been defined as a requirement to take reasonable care to avoid acts or omissions which can be reasonably foreseen as likely to injure persons who are closely or directly affected by those acts or omissions. Where an injury occurs and this leads to a civil claim or criminal prosecution, it is for the court to decide what was reasonable in the particular circumstances of the case. The stalker's best defence is to be able to show that he did everything necessary to keep the risks as low as reasonably practicable.

Risk assessment

The law requires risk assessments to be completed and retained in writing. Properly done and acted upon, they are the stalker's and owner or occupier's best protection against prosecution.

In a nutshell, risk assessment consists of isolating activities, seeing who might be harmed by them and identifying the control measures that will be needed to ensure that each hazard is as low as reasonably practicable. In addition, isolating each individual activity enables a check to be made of whether particular statutory requirements apply to it and whether the duty owed is more specific than keeping the risk as low as reasonably practicable.

There are several ways of quantifying the risks of a particular activity but the important thing is to keep the analysis as simple as possible. The Health and Safety Executive suggests a simple table in which the likelihood of an injury and its possible severity are scored. Multiplied together, these scores produce a total that can be used as an indication of whether any action is required and, if so, what. For example:

Score	Likelihood	Severity
0	Negligible	No injury
1	Very unlikely	First aid only
2	Unlikely	Minor injury
3	Probable	Three-day injury
4	Very likely	Major injury
5	Almost certain	Disabling or fatal

The next step is to check the result of multiplying the scores for likelihood and severity against an action table. For example:

Risk Score	Action
0–1	No action required.
2–6	Record the risk and keep it as low as practicable.
7–16	Record the risk and add further controls to reduce it.
17–24	Consider stopping the activity until essential controls are in place and seek advice
25	Stop the activity immediately and seek advice.

To illustrate the use of this method of assessment, consider a visiting stalker taking a shot towards woods that conceal a footpath on which the public has right of way. There is a risk that walkers using the footpath or wandering in the woods will be injured by a misdirected shot. In the absence of controls, this risk might be rated as follows:

$$\text{Very likely (4)} \times \text{Fatal (5)} = 20$$

The required action will be to stop the activity until essential controls are in place and seek advice. The required controls might include:

- providing the visiting stalker with a detailed briefing on the hazard
- prohibiting shooting unless there is a solid earth stop behind the target (this might require a high seat to be erected)
- ensuring that the right of way is properly signed and that signs warning walkers to keep out of the woods are in place

In deciding on the controls that are required, full account must be taken of the possible ages of walkers using the right of way and of the stalker's age and experience.

As a second example, consider the risk of leaving a defective high seat in a place where children might be tempted to play on it. Depending on where the high seat is, this might be rated as:

$$\text{Probable (3)} \times \text{Major injury (4)} = 12$$

The required action will be to record the risk and add controls to reduce it. These might include:

- repairing or replacing the high seat and maintaining an inspection record
- moving it to a place where it is less likely to tempt children
- adding a sign (which children can understand) warning unauthorised people not to climb into the seat or tamper with it

From these two examples, it will be seen that there is nothing very startling about risk assessment. Apart from the fact that it is a legal requirement, it is a simple, disciplined and effective way of thinking through all the risks of deer stalking and devising controls that keep them as low as reasonably practicable. Keeping a file of written assessments together with their associated briefing notes and updating them regularly ensures that risk controls respond sensibly to changing circumstances. In addition to a regular cycle of review, risk assessments must be reviewed whenever there is an incident and the new written assessment must be added to the file.

If an injury does occur, the person investigating it will make very detailed inquiries into the system of risk assessment that was in place, the assessment of the particular risk that gave rise to the injury and the action that was taken to keep the risk as low as reasonably practicable. The fact that there was an injury is likely to lead him to the conclusion that something was not as well or accurately done as it might have been. If, however, the evidence, including the written risk assessment record, convinces him that, in the circumstances as they were seen at the time, everything reasonable was done to avoid the injury, he is likely to conclude in the end that it was an accident. For all concerned, this will be the best possible outcome from a thoroughly regrettable incident.

Stalkers and food safety

A stalker who shoots a deer, dresses the carcass and sells it to a game dealer is producing and selling food. Like everybody else involved in the food chain, he is subject to the Food Safety Act 1990, which establishes four criminal offences:

- selling or possessing for sale food that does not meet food safety requirements
- rendering food injurious to health
- selling food that is not of the nature, substance and quality demanded
- falsely or misleadingly describing or presenting food

The penalties for these offences are potentially very severe; they can include imprisonment and very heavy fines. The main way in which stalkers will avoid incurring them will be to obey the **Food Safety (General Food Hygiene) Regulations 1995**. These regulations are enforced by the Environmental Health Departments of local authorities. As they apply to uncooked wild game meat (e.g. carcasses sold by stalkers to game dealers), the recommended minimum standards required by the regulations are clarified by the L.A.C.O.T.S. publication *Wild Game 1997*. Responsible stalkers will possess their own copies of the Regulations and the L.A.C.O.T.S. publication.

Most recreational stalkers will dress the deer they themselves have shot. In some cases, this will be done entirely in the field and the carcass will be taken straight to a game dealer. In other cases, some or all of the work will be done in an estate larder and the carcass may remain there for some time before it goes to the dealer. What follows is intended only as a guide to stalkers. It covers neither the responsibilities of the owner or occupier of the land nor the detailed requirements for the construction and operation of his larder.

After the shooting of a deer but before it is introduced into the food chain, it is necessary to ensure that:

- there is no evidence that the animal was diseased
- the carcass has not become contaminated

Recreational stalkers are rarely experts in animal diseases but, with training and experience, they are well able to recognise when something is wrong. When a stalker does see an abnormality, he should not go on poking about with his knife. He must stop and:

- if he suspects the presence of a notifiable disease, report it immediately to the Police, M.A.F.F. (or S.O.A.E.F.D. in Scotland), the Divisional Veterinary Officer, the Animal Health Inspector and, in the case of anthrax, the Consultant in Communicable Disease Control
- in all other cases, record the abnormality and report it to the game dealer to whom the carcass is sold (and, possibly, seek the advice of a veterinary surgeon)

The notifiable diseases of deer are bovine tuberculosis, foot and mouth disease and anthrax.

As far as contamination is concerned, the stalker must carefully consider every step between his shot and his offer to sell the carcass to a game dealer. Starting at the beginning:

- It is recommended that wild deer should be shot in either the neck or the chest.
- After checking that it is dead and without touching it in any other way, the stalker should conduct an external examination of the dead animal.
- Satisfied that there is no external evidence of disease, he must immediately bleed the carcass by severing the main blood vessels at the top of the heart. This is done by inserting a knife at the sticking point.

What happens thereafter requires a certain amount of judgement:

- If he is reasonably close to a larder that can be operated hygienically, he should go there to complete the work of dressing the carcass. This is because the larder will provide a controlled environment in which the risk of contamination is kept as low as reasonably practicable.
- If the time taken to reach the larder will be unduly long, and particularly if the weather is warm, he should at least remove the animal's abdominal contents (gralloch it) in the field. The place in which this is done should be chosen to minimise the risk of contamination and the animal dragged or carried there in a way that also minimises the risk – for example, by using a drag bag or roe sack.
- If the animal is gralloched in the field, most stalkers will wish to remove its red offal (pluck) and possibly its head at the same time.
- If the gralloched carcass is to be left unattended for more than a few minutes, it should be suspended from a tree and enclosed in a fly-proof net that does not impede the free circulation of air.

At whatever stage carcasses are transported to the larder or game dealer, the vehicles and containers that are used should be clean and disinfected. and any drag bags used must be regularly inspected and cleaned.

Whether the carcass is dressed in a larder or in the field, great care must be taken to prevent the meat from becoming contaminated by:

- the contents of its bladder, stomach and intestines
- material adhering to its coat
- material transferred from the stalker's person or clothing
- other environmental material including animal dung, agricultural chemicals and insects

All of these risks can be kept as low as reasonably practicable by using appropriate dressing techniques and equipment:

- Having recovered and bled the dead animal, a stalker who intends to dress it in the field should first ensure that his outer clothing is not contaminated. He should remove it if, for example, he has crawled across a field on which farmyard manure has recently been spread!
- He should next wash his hands using clean, potable water (that is, drinkable water). If his practice is to use water from a container for this purpose, he should ensure that it is fresh and that its container is regularly cleaned and sterilised. Any cuts or abrasions on his hands should be covered with clean, waterproof dressings and he should dry them with a clean, disposable paper towel.
- Most experienced stalkers now cover their hands with disposable gloves. This not only prevents contamination of the carcass by the stalker; it also

protects the stalker from any infection that the carcass might harbour. Latex examination gloves are quite all right except that they are easily punctured. Vinyl gloves are less easily damaged and easier to keep clean. Care must be taken to ensure that gloves carried in a pocket remain sterile before they are used – putting them in a small freezer bag is quite a good idea.

- The next step is for the stalker to take hold of his knife. Its blade should be very sharp (for the stalker's own safety); it should be so designed that the risk of puncturing the animal's stomach or intestine is minimised; its handle should be made from a material that can easily be cleaned and sterilised. and the attachment between handle and blade should be so designed that it does not harbour contamination. Taken together, these requirements rule out folding knives and knives with handles made of wood, bone or other absorbent materials.
- The stalker next proceeds to the first stage of dressing the carcass. There are several equally good gralloching procedures. Nearly all start by cutting around and freeing the anus and external reproductive organs so that, with the rectum, they can be cleanly withdrawn through the pelvic girdle. Care must be taken not to puncture the bladder at this stage. The next step is to open the abdomen from aitchbone to the sternum (breastbone) with a single clean cut, taking great care not to puncture the stomach or intestines.
- What follows depends on whether or not the red offal (pluck) is to be removed at the same time as the gralloch. If so, the cut should be continued over the breastbone to the sticking point and carried straight on to a point just behind the lower jaw. In the smaller species or very young animals, a sharp knife can then be used to open the chest cavity by cutting the breast bone. Otherwise, the breastbone must be sawn open throughout its length. If possible, the carcass should now be suspended. Starting at its hind end, the entire contents of its abdomen, chest and throat can then easily be removed in a single piece. The process is completed by cutting away the windpipe and oesophagus close behind the lower jaw.
- If only the gralloch is to be removed, only the abdomen and throat should be opened. The oesophagus is then freed from the windpipe and knotted to prevent the escape of stomach contents. Having cleared it of connective tissue around the sticking point and as it emerges through the diaphragm, the oesophagus can be withdrawn towards the hind end of the carcass and cleared away with the contents of the abdomen.

At whatever stage the contents of the chest and abdomen are removed, they must be checked for signs of disease. This particularly applies to the gralloch which, in many cases, will be buried in the field. The stomach, intestines and mesenteric lymph nodes must be examined. If disease is suspected, they must be bagged up and taken with the carcass for expert examination. The same applies to any suspicion of disease arising from the stalker's inspection of the pluck. In any case, it is good practice to keep the pluck and, if possible, the head with the carcass and offer it to the game dealer who buys it. When this is done, a system of tamper-proof tags identifying the pluck and head with the carcass is recommended.

After dressing an animal that has been shot in the chest, it is often necessary to wipe blood from the interior surfaces of its rib cage and throat. This is best done by using disposable, sterile, absorbent paper. The paper used in dairies is ideal and the required quantity can easily be kept in a pocket. Like disposable gloves, it should be protected from contamination by keeping it in a small freezer bag.

Where the contents of the stomach, intestines or bladder have contaminated the meat some cleaning to prevent the contamination from spreading may be necessary. The temptation to erase the evidence by wiping or washing it completely away must, however, be resisted. The effort is very unlikely to be entirely successful and attempting to sell the carcass without warning the buyer of what has happened may risk prosecution for at least two offences against the Food Safety Act.

Finally, having taken all reasonable steps to prepare an uncontaminated carcass for sale, the stalker must take care to prevent it from deteriorating before it has been delivered to the dealer. It should be hung with sufficient space to allow air to circulate freely around it in a cool place that is proof against insects and other contaminants. If its temperature cannot be progressively reduced to and maintained at 7°C, steps must be taken to get it to the game dealer as quickly as possible.

Some useful publications

Health and Safety at Work Act 1974
Animal Health Act 1981
Food Safety Act 1990
Management of Health and Safety at Work Regulations 1992
Young Persons (Health and Safety at Work) Regulations 1997
Provision and Use of Work Equipment Regulations 1992
Manual Handling Operations Regulations 1992
Personal Protective Equipment Regulations 1992
Agriculture (Ladders) Regulations
Agriculture (Lifting of Heavy Weights) Regulations
All Terrain Vehicles (Safety) Regulations 1989
The Food Safety(General Food Hygiene) Regulations 1995
Guide to Reporting of Injuries, Diseases and Dangerous Occurrences 1985
Wild Game 1997, L.A.C.O.T.S.
Chain Saws, H.S.E. AS5
Health and Safety (Safety Signs and Signals) Regulations 1996

Index